What's Your Poison?
How Cocktails Got Their Names

By Jerry Bader

What's Your Poison?
How Cocktails Got Their Names

Written by Jerry Bader
Illustrated by Dream Computer
Produced by MRPwebmedia.com/books

For Gail, who wanted to know how cocktails got their names.

What's Your Poison?
How Cocktails Got Their Names

By Jerry Bader

Why do we call mixed alcohol drinks "cocktails"? How do they get their exotic names: names like the Singapore Sling, Screw Driver, the Alamagoozlum, the Angel's Kiss, the Hanky Panky, the Harvey Wallbanger, Sex On The Beach, the Monkey Gland, the Brass Monkey, the Margarita, the Japalac, the Lion's Tail, and many, many more?

Who makes up these names, where are they invented, why, and how do you make them? These questions will be answered in "What's Your Poison?" by exploring the incidents, people, and places that prompted the creation of these exotic concoctions.

Table of Contents

- The Jack Rose
- The Cock's Tail
- Why cocktails are called cocktails.
- The Egg Cup
- The Sazerac
- The Rooster and The Dregs
- The Bobbed Tail
- The Gimlet
- The Mojito
- The Cuban Trifecta
- The Daiquiri
- The Fu Manchu Daiquiri
- The Gin and Tonic
- The Cuba Libre
- Monkey Business
- The Brass Monkey
- The Monkey Gland
- Monkey 47
- Monkeys Gone Bad
- The Margarita Mystery
- The Tom Collins Hoax of 1894
- Cocktails of New York's Five Boroughs
- The Manhattan
- The Bronx
- The Brooklyn
- The Queens
- The Staten Island
- The Harvey Wallbanger
- The Earthquake and The Artist

- Absinthe
- The French Method
- The Bohemian Method
- The Experience
- Cabaret de L'Enfer
- Cabaret du Néant
- The Giger Bar
- The Negroni
- The Singapore Sling
- Cocktails Named After Sex
- The Hanky Panky
- The White Lady and Duelling Harries
- Sex On The Beach
- Long Island Ice Tea
- Irish Coffee
- Screech
- Cocktails That Will Burn Your House Down
- The Flaming Giraffe
- The Flaming S'more Martini
- The Cotton Candy Martini
- The Angel's Kiss
- Forgotten Gems
- The Leatherneck
- The Lion's Tail
- The Japalac
- The Twelve-Mile Limit
- The Alamagoozlum
- The Name Game
- Random Cocktail Recipes

The Mariner's Ghost, The Nut Bunny, The Trojan Horse, The Tiger Paw, The Red Dragon's Breath, The Salty Dog, The Bulldog Smash, Espresso Martini, Tokyo Tea, The Last Word

Baldy Jack Rose

1
The Jack Rose

A Bald Gambler, A Corrupt Police Detective, A Murdered Casino Owner, And A Dash of Applejack

New York City, July 16, 1912, it's a hot steamy afternoon. Four men wait under the awning of the Hotel Metropole located at 147 West 43rd Street. The hotel is a five story brick building on the corner close to Times Square. A sign above and to the side of the canopy over the entrance tells visitors they've arrived at the famous Metropole, the first hotel in New York City with running water in every room, home to gambler Nicky Arnstein, Fanny Brice's lover and ultimate second husband, Bat Masterson, ex-western lawman, now New York City sports' writer, and Herman Rosenthal, bookmaker and illegal casino owner.

The four men milling about outside the hotel are not out of place on the busy street. They're wearing summer weight suits suitable for the weather. Jacob, Whitey Lewis, Seidenschner wears his usual cloth flat-cap, while Francisco Cirofici, aka Dago Frank, Harry Horowitz, aka Gyp the Blood, and Lefty Louie Rosenberg, all wear straw boater's, a popular male fashion statement of the time.

These men are all members of the Lennox Avenue Gang led by Harry Horowitz and controlled by Zelig Harry Lefkowitz, aka Jack Zelig, head of the Eastman Gang. The Lennox Avenue group could be considered the prototype of the more famous criminal gang known as Murder Incorporated.

As Herman Rosenthal exits the front door of the Metropole the four men surround him, draw their guns and fire. Gambler Herman Rosenthal is shot dead in broad daylight on a crowded New York street. As Rosenthal lies bleeding on the pavement the four men scramble to the waiting car provided by Baldy Jack Rose, the man who hired them to murder Rosenthal on orders from crooked NYPD Lieutenant Charles Becker.

Baldy Jack Rose was born Jacob Rosenzweig in Poland in 1876. His family immigrated to America and at the age of four Rosenzweig was stricken with typhoid leaving him with *alopecia universalis*, a condition causing all his hair to fall out. Cruel classmates teased Jacob giving him the nickname Baldy, an apparent prerequisite for a life of crime as all the gangsters in this tale seem to have colourful monikers, and Baldy Jack Rose seemed appropriately fitting for a hairless young criminal.

Baldy spent his early years in Connecticut where he grew up to be a gambler, boxing promoter, and founder of a minor league baseball team, The Rosebuds, not the toughest sounding name for a sports team owned by the man that became embroiled in one of America's most infamous murders. If not for being overshadowed by Lucky Luciano's bloody rise to power, the Rosenthal murder might be regarded as New York City's most infamous gangland murder.

After moving to New York City, Rose opened an illegal casino called The Rosebud. It wasn't long before it became an underworld hangout, especially favored by the Eastman Gang headed by Selig Harry Lefkowitz, and its offshoot the Lennox Avenue Gang led by Harry, Gyp The Blood, Horowitz.

Unfortunately for Baldy, NYPD Lieutenant Charles Becker and his Gambling Squad eventually raided The Rosebud. Becker used the opportunity to extort a weekly twenty-five percent protection levy from Baldy, amounting to a substantial ten thousand dollar a month payout; a payment that Baldy Jack Rose chalked up to the cost of doing business in New York City.

If that wasn't bad enough Becker demanded Baldy collect payments from the other illegal gambling casinos he was shaking down. One of these casinos was run by Herman Rosenthal, a man less inclined to pay Becker what he demanded. Rosenthal went so far as to complain to District Attorney Charles S. Whitman, an odd thing to do for a man that ran an illegal gambling club, but never the less that is what he did, in writing, signing an affidavit that was published in the *New York World* newspaper. A couple of days after Rosenthal's meeting with Whitman, Rosenthal was gunned down in front of the Hotel Metropole.

The hit was messy, witnessed by numerous passersby. Baldy figured it was only a matter of time before he would be caught so instead he went to the police and admitted his involvement in hiring Selig's Lenox Avenue boys as well as arranging for the get-away car on orders from NYPD Lieutenant Charles Becker. Jacob Seidenschner, Francisco Cirofici, Harry Horowitz, Lefty Louie Rosenberg, and Charles Becker were all arrested, convicted, and ultimately electrocuted at Sing Sing Correctional Facility based on the testimony of Baldy Jack Rose. Zelig Harry Lefkowitz, aka, Jack Zelig, The Big Yid, leader of the Eastman Gang and the Lenox Avenue boys also cut a deal but was gunned down on October 5th, 1912 the day before he was supposed to testify in court.

Baldy Jack Rose managed to escape gangland retribution and went on to earn a thousand dollars a week lecturing about the evils of gambling on vaudeville stages and in church basements. He even appeared in a few motion pictures. He retired to Connecticut where he farmed for a while, eventually moving back to New York City where he died October 4th, 1947.

Thus ends the tale of Baldy Jack Rose – well almost – this is a book about cocktails after all, and so it is said the Jack Rose Cocktail is named after the infamous Baldy Jack Rose. Now you may never have heard of the Jack Rose cocktail as it has fallen out of favor in recent years, but there was a time when it was considered one of the six basic cocktails as cited in David Embury's *The Fine Art of Mixing Drinks* (1948). Like most cocktail names the legend behind the name is disputed. Some say the Jack Rose is really named after the rose color provided by the Applejack used in making the drink, but that is hardly as interesting as the tale of the alopecia plagued gambler. And who's to say that both explanations aren't true.

One final word on Baldy Jack Rose: there are those that suggest Charles Becker was innocent of involvement in the Rosenthal murder and that he was setup by Rose and his associates, probably payback for Becker's extortion racket. The truth as is often the case is lost to history.

The Jack Rose Cocktail

According to drinkstraightup.com, *The Straight Up, Pre-Prohibition Cocktails and Modern Twists On Classics*, the Jack Rose is a 'light and fruity cocktail' with a surprising 'tart' edge held in check by the sweet grenadine.

How To Make A Jack Rose Cocktail

1. Pour 2 oz of Applejack into a shaker.
2. Add .75 oz of Lime Juice.
3. Add .5 oz of Grenadine.
4. Add ice.
5. Shake well.
6. Strain into a chilled cocktail glass and serve.

The Rosebud Cocktail

I can't say the Rosebud was named after Baldy Jack Rose, maybe it's a reference to the movie *Citizen Kane*, but whatever the truth, it's a good excuse to start telling the story of the infamous criminal. This is the simplest version of the Rosebud that I came across.

How To Make A Rosebud Cocktail

1. Half-fill a shaker with ice.
2. Add 2 oz of Citrus Vodka.
3. Add .5 oz of Triple Sec.
4. Add 1 oz of Lemon Juice.
5. Add 2 oz of Grapefruit Juice to ice-filled Collins Glass.
6. Shake and Strain into the Collins Glass and serve.

2
The Cock's Tale
The Carousel Bar, French Quarter, New Orleans

People are sitting at the famous rotating circular Carousel Bar in the Hotel Monteleone. The ornately decorated canopy over the bar features eight court jesters surrounded by round light bulbs while the backs of the carved barstool display images of brightly colored circus animals. The bartender approaches, "What's your poison?" The customer orders a Sazerac, the official cocktail of New Orleans as voted by the Louisiana House of Representatives.

The Sazerac is arguably the first cocktail; perhaps the legendary reason we call cocktails, cocktails, a combination of ingredients created not far from the Carousel Bar & Lounge in an apothecary shop on Royal Street owned by a Saint-Dominique transplant named Antoine Peychaud in 1838.

Perhaps it's never crossed your mind why cocktails are called cocktails or why they have such colorful names. Perhaps like me, you don't even drink, but alcohol has played a significant role in history, a history that is fascinating, controversial, and in some cases influential.

Who were these people who came up with fanciful concoctions like the Singapore Sling, the Angel's Kiss, the Redheaded Slut, Sex On The Beach, Fat Like Buddha, or the somewhat lengthy, A Lonely Island Lost In The Middle Of A Foggy Sea? And that's just a few of the fabulous drinks that we call cocktails. It seems many of these drinks like the Jack Rose have a story to tell; and what's better when indulging in a fine liquid refreshment than discussing the veracity of how it came into being.

But before we dive into where, how, and who came up with these wacky names, we have to answer the question: why do we call cocktails, cocktails? Unfortunately the answer isn't as straightforward as you would hope, but then again if truth and facts were always the same, it would be a very dull and boring world. Like most everything else, the history of the cocktail is a malleable tale of people, places, and legendary circumstance.

3
The Eggcup
A French Quarter Apothecary Shop Circa 1838

The walls are lined with ornate scalloped wooden shelves containing numerous glass bottles and jars with labels indicating their contents. The shelves are divided into sections by faux-columns topped with decorated porcelain jars. The shelves sit atop matching wooden cabinets with multiple small medicine drawers. In front of the display of inventory is a scalloped counter also containing numerous small drawers that hold the magic potions and remedies sold. On either end of the counter are bronze sculptures depicting Asclepius the Greek god of medicine. The man standing behind the counter is dressed in gray trousers, a paisley double-breasted collared-vest, a billowy black silk cravat, and a white shirt with a stand-up butterfly collar. He is Antoine Amédée Peychaud, a new arrival in New Orleans from the French Colony of Saint-Dominique, now Haiti, and this is his apothecary shop.

"Excuse me, Monsieur Peychaud but I understand you claim to be the inventor of the cocktail."

Peychaud: "Oui Monsieur, the cocktail as you call it is my invention."

"But why did you call it a cocktail?"

Peychaud: "To be precise, Monsieur, I invented the Sazerac, a combination of Sazerac brandy and my own special brand of Peychaud Bitters."

"But where does the word cocktail come from?"

Peychaud: "The word is *coquetier*, in English... eggcup. I mix the brandy and bitters in a *coquetier* to serve it. People mispronounce the word, so gradually *coquetier* became known as cocktail, *voila l'histoire.*"

If Monsieur Peychaud's story is true, the first cocktail is the Sazerac, the official cocktail of New Orleans. There's no doubt the Sazerac is one tasty beverage, but is it the first cocktail, and is his eggcup serving shtick the reason we call cocktails, cocktails?

Here's the problem, Monsieur Peychaud came up with his little eggcup refreshment around 1838, but the term cocktail as applied to mixed drinks was already in use. In fact, a definition of the word cocktail as applied to mixed drinks can be found in the May 13, 1806 edition of *The Balance and Columbian Repository*, not the catchiest name for a periodical I've ever heard, but still there it is.

In 1806 Peychaud was still a small boy too young to coin the term cocktail. And so we have to look a little harder if we want the real story behind the origin of the cocktail, but at least Monsieur Peychaud can be credited with the creation of the Sazerac cocktail and Peychaud Bitters.

The Sazerac
The Official Cocktail of New Orleans

New Orleans seems to be the birthplace of numerous cocktails. In addition to the Sazerac, the Brandy Crusta, the Brandy Milk Punch, the Absinthe Frappé, the Ramos Gin Fizz, the Café Brulot, the Roffignac, and the Hurricane were all created in New Orleans.

How To Make A Sazerac
1. Drop a sugar cube into a mixing glass with just enough water to get it moist; then crush the cube with the back of a spoon.
2. Add 1.5 oz of Rye Whiskey. The original Sazerac used imported French cognac from *Sazerac-du-Forge et Fils*, but most bartenders today use Rye.
3. Add 2 dashes of Peychaud's Bitters.
4. Add 1 dash of Angostura Bitters.
5. Let the mixture chill for a bit.
6. Coat the sides of an Old Fashion Glass with 1 teaspoon of Absinthe, Pernod, or Hebsaint if you want it New Orleans style.
7. Pour out the excess that remains.
8. Strain the Rye mixture into the coated glass.
9. Finish by squeezing a Lemon Peel over the glass, rub it around the rim, and drop it into the glass, *voilà* the Sazerac.

4
The Rooster and Dregs
The Backroom Of A 19th Century Saloon

The room is littered with wooden barrels. Two workmen both wearing white work shirts, woollen vests, and pants covered by stained aprons take their afternoon break. One man leans up against a stack of barrels drinking from a mug while the other sits on a barrel enjoying his beverage.

"I understand you're making cocktails." The men laugh. They speak in Boston Irish accents.

Worker One: "Don't be a chucklehead. There's no such thing as a cocktail."

Worker Two: "Don't be daft Charlie-boy, he's talking about cock-tailings."

Worker One: "Then why don't he say so. These fancy gentlemen types should learn to speak the language."

"Well... can you tell me exactly what you're doing?"

Worker Two: "We're taking the dregs or tailings, the nasty bits left in the bottom of the almost empty barrels and adding them together so they can be sold."

Worker One: "Sold at a discount, mind you."

"So that's the tailings part of the cock-tailings but where does the cock part come from?"

"Worker One: "You don't know much do ya sir? You'd think a fine-spoken fellow like yourself would be more knowledgeable about such things. A man that don't know about cocks is a strange man indeed."

Both men chuckle, Worker Two holds up one of the stoppers that are used to plug the hole in the barrel where the whiskey comes out.

Worker Two: "This here is a cock my friend, also the spigot used to serve the whiskey is called a cock. And so the discounted mixture made from the remains is called cock-tailings."

It's easy to understand how the term cock-tailings quickly turned into cocktails: a way for bar owners to sell the inferior dregs from the bottom of the barrels, certainly a plausible explanation of the word's origin. Another variation of the story had bartenders using Rooster-shaped spigots on the barrels of the cock-tailings so customers would know which barrels contained the discounted alcohol. There are even stories of saloonkeepers dumping the alcohol dregs into ceramic jars shaped like roosters with the discounted drinks dispensed by pressing the tail of the cock, but then some people say the term, cocktail, came from the practice of bobbing the tails of mix breed horses.

5
The Bobbed Tail

A Stable With A Groom Brushing A Horse With A Bobbed Tail

Groom: "Evening friend, how can I be of service?"

"I understand the term cocktail has something to do with horses. Do know anything about that?"

Groom: "You see the tail on Dusty here, it's bobbed or cocked if you prefer, letting people know Dusty isn't a thoroughbred. The idea that horses of mixed breeding were distinguished from pure breeds by their cocked tails became a popular term for anything of mixed or inferior origin; be it a gentleman who lacked a proper pedigree, or an alcoholic beverage of inferior mixed contents, and so the cocked tail became the cocktail."

Perhaps we'll never know the exact origin of the word cocktail, perhaps the word has multiple origins, or perhaps it's fitting that its beginnings remain ambiguous, especially when we consider it's the name we apply to a class of beverages steeped in mystery, intrigue, and whimsy. Take for example the Gimlet, a refreshing tangy mixture of gin and lime juice.

Raymond Chandler

6
The Gimlet
The HMS Warrior Gun Deck Mess

Several seamen sit eating and drinking from metal plates and mugs. Between each mess table is a large Armstrong muzzle loaded cannon. A variety of wooden buckets hang from metal rods in the ceiling along with rolled up and tightly bound hammocks used for sleeping. All in all the space is practical and efficient. The men are dressed in classic mid eighteen hundred Royal Navy seamen attire.

"I see you boys are enjoying a beverage. Can you tell me exactly what it is?"

Sailor One: "This here is Mr. Lauchlin Rose's Lime Juice, made special for His Majesty's sailor boys because it doesn't need to be refrigerated. It's a tangy source of Vitamin C that helps the boys avoid the scourge of scurvy."

One of the sailors passes a flask to the first sailor who pours some of its contents into his metal mug. Sailor One then passes the flask along to the others who all top-up their mugs with the contents of the flask.

Sailor Two: "Aye, and a wee bit extra ingredient to warm the belly." The men laugh.

"And what are you adding to the lime juice?"

Sailor One takes a swig from the flask then wipes his mouth with his sleeve. He then pours a little extra into his mug. "This here, my friend, is gin." He holds up the metal mug containing the mixture. "It gives Mr. Rose's lime juice a little bite. A gimlet we call it."

"And why do you call it a gimlet?"

Sailor Two takes a pointed metal auger from his pocket and stabs it into the wooden table. "It's a tasty drink with a sharp pointed edge to it, like the sharp pointy bit at the end of this here gimlet used to drill holes."

Of course when it comes to cocktails, if one explanation is good, two is even better. In this case some attribute the naming of the Gimlet to British Royal Navy Surgeon Rear-Admiral Sir Thomas Gimlette KCB, who is said to have introduced the anti-scurvy medication to his fellow officers in the late nineteenth century, however the remedy had already been in use by the Royal Navy as early as the mid eighteenth century.

Perhaps Sir Gimlette and his friends were the ones to add the right touch of class to the mixture, taking it from the gun deck mess to mainstream society. The more widespread popularity of the Gimlet can be traced back to pulp fiction author Raymond Chandler, who mentions the Gimlet in *The Long Goodbye* as Phillip Marlowe's favorite thirst quencher when chasing down a hot lead or a delicious dame.

The Gimlet

A Tasty Medicinal Preventative

The Gimlet is not the only cocktail that found its way into our hearts and bellies by way of the sea as a means to prevent disease, but first let's find out how to create a classic Gimlet.

How To Make A Gimlet

1. Add 2 oz of Gin to a cocktail shaker.
2. Add .75 oz of Rose's Lime Juice (some people prefer equal parts Gin and Rose's Lime Juice).
3. Fill the shaker with ice and shake well.
4. Strain into a Cocktail Glass.
5. Garnish with a Lime Wedge. If Gin is not your thing, you can substitute Vodka.

Ernest Hemingway

7
The Mojito
La Bodeguita del Medio, Havana Cuba

Havana, Cuba, a narrow side street with a brightly colored vintage mid-1950 Chevy parked in front of the La Bodeguita del Medio, restaurant and bar. The sound of Latin music mixed with laughter and animated conversations spills out onto the street. The place is not fancy. Behind the bar the shelves are lined with an endless number of bottles. The walls are covered in scribbled autographs and messages behind numerous framed posters, photographs, and memorabilia, including a large painting of Ernest Hemingway and a framed handwritten note signed by Hemingway that reads: *"My mojito in La Bodeguita, My daiquiri in El Floridita."* La Bodeguita del Medio was one of Hemingway's favorite watering holes, and it is said that he had a particular fondness for Mojitos.

Like the Gimlet, the Mojito has its origins as a way for sailors to prevent scurvy. And like most things involving a seamen's life, if something was good, adding more booze could only make it better.

After his successful raid on Cartagena de Indias, Francis Drake sailed to Havana where his men sought out a local Indian remedy for scurvy caused by the lack of Vitamin C in their diets. The ingredients included *aguardiente de cana*, an early form of rum, mixed with lime, sugarcane juice, and mint. Although the mixture was not called a Mojito, it did contain the basic ingredients we associate with the drink.

The Mojito

A High Balling Kind Of Cocktail

The Mojito name may have derived from the word *mojo*, a seasoning made from limes, although there are other explanations. Some say the name derives from the Spanish, *mojaditio*, meaning 'a little wet.' The Mojito is traditionally served in a highball glass that itself has a bit of an interesting etymology: a highball being any mixed drink that has an alcohol base, mixed with a larger quantity of non-alcoholic mixers, and served in a tall glass. The term highball used to describe the tall glass and type of cocktail used to fill it, originally came from the painted white ball on a raised pole, signalling train engineers that the track ahead was clear. The signal gave the conductor permission to proceed at full throttle, hence the term "high balling."

How To Make A Mojito

1. Add 6 mint leaves, 1 oz of fresh Lime Juice, and 2 teaspoons of sugar, to a shaker. Crush and mix the ingredients together using a muddler (a tool used to mash).
2. Add 1.5 oz of White Rum.
3. Pour into a Highball Glass over ice.
4. Fill with Soda Water.
5. Garnish with a Mint Sprig.
6. Serve with a straw.

The Gimlet and the Mojito are not the only cocktails inspired by a mix of Cuban culture, sailor thirst, scurvy, lime, and alcohol.

8
The Cuban Trifecta
The Pink-Painted El Floridita Bar, Havana Cuba

If the La Bodeguita del Medio is famous for the Mojito and Ernest Hemingway, then the El Floridita is as famous for Mr. Hemmingway and the Daiquiri. In 1817, La Pina de Plata, The Silver Pineapple, opened where the El Floridita now stands. By about 1917 the name was changed to El Florida, eventually transitioning into the current El Floridita. In 1918 Constantino Ribalaigua Vert a bartender, or *cantinero*, became the owner. Sometime in the 1930s Constantino invented the Daiquiri, a favorite of frequent visitor Ernest Hemmingway when he wasn't at La Bodeguita. It wasn't long before El Floridita became known as *"la cuna del daiquiri,"* the cradle of the daiquiri, as is proudly displayed on the neon sign that hangs over the street corner entrance.

The exterior of the restaurant bar is painted an eye-catching pink. The quaint rustic chaos of the La Bodeguita is replaced with a more elegant effort in the El Floridita, despite the limitation of Caribbean heat and a depressed economy. Behind the bar is a long red refrigerated cabinet with multiple red doors trimmed in black. Over the cabinets is a large muted landscape mural surrounded by a wide polished dark stained wood moulding. The *cantineros* or bartenders are dressed in white shirts and pants with red aprons and ties. The tables surrounding the parquet dance floor feature white tablecloths with red overclothes surrounded by fancy wrought iron chairs. If a Daiquiri is what you desire, then El Floridita is the place to have it.

Teddy Roosevelt

9
The Daiquiri
A Spoon Full Of Cane Sugar Makes The Medicine Go Down

Following Teddy Roosevelt's victory at San Juan Hill, American business interests started to exploit Cuban iron-ore resources. One of the engineers sent to look into the mining opportunities was Jennings Cox, a stout fellow who wore rimless glasses and slick-backed hair parted in the middle. To help ease the hardships of frontier life, Cox demanded each of his men receive a daily ration of local Bacardi Carta Blanca rum. Cox noticed that the locals mixed the rum with their coffee, so he started experimenting with various mixtures using the Carta Blanca as the alcohol base. Cox and another engineer named Pagliuchi, met one evening and decided to see what they could come up with using the ingredients they had on hand, rum, limes, and sugar. The result is what has become known as the Daiquiri.

According to Basil Woon in his 1928 book, "When It's Cocktail Time in Cuba," Cox and his colleagues met every morning in Santiago, at the Venus Bar, to knock-back three or four of his rum and lime concoctions for breakfast. I suppose there's nothing like starting a hard day's work at the mines half in the bag, but these were frontier men so you'll have to cut them some slack.

One morning, so the legend goes, Cox suggested that their favorite morning pick-me-up should be given a proper name.

Cox suggested that since they all worked at the Daiquiri mine, the new rum mixture should henceforth be called the Daiquiri. In 1902 US Congressman William A. Chandler, owner of the mine, discovered Cox's creation, and introduced it to New Yorkers. The Daiquiri was able to reach an even wider audience when in 1909 Admiral Lucius Johnson delighted his fellow soldiers at the Army Navy Club in Washington, DC by introducing them to the new cocktail.

The Daiquiri
Although the ingredients of the Daiquiri have remained consistent over the years, its preparation has been altered over time. It is no longer served in a tall highball glass filled with ice as it was in the early 1900s but instead is delivered in a Martini glass.

How To Make A Daiquiri
1. Add 1 teaspoon of sugar into a cocktail shaker.
2. Add .75 oz of freshly squeezed Lime Juice.
3. Stir until the sugar is dissolved.
4. Add 2 oz of Light Rum.
5. Fill shaker with ice and shake well.
6. Strain into a chilled Martini Glass.
7. Garnish with a Lime Wedge.

Jennings Cox

10
The Fu Manchu Daiquiri

There are numerous Daiquiri variations, however one of the more obscure versions, the Fu Manchu, deserves a mention. According to biographer Cay Van Ash, while on a trip to Jamaica in 1932, British author Sax Rohmer visited the Myers Rum Distillery. Rohmer and his entourage spent the morning trying to come up with a new cocktail presumably to help promote his books. The task turned out to be more challenging than was necessary since Rohmer insisted the new cocktail must have a mysterious green color. After fourteen attempts, presumably sampling each one, the men were in no condition to have their scheduled lunch, or to engage in any activity that involved standing up.

The reason Rohmer insisted the color of the drink had to be a mysterious green shade was because it was to be named after the fictional evil villain in his popular books, the diabolical Dr. Fu Manchu. Rohmer had already established his villain's signature moustache as the Fu Manchu, so why not a cocktail featuring the same shade of green silk his character often donned?

How To Make A Fu Manchu
1. Fill a shaker with ice.
2. Add 1.5 oz of Dark Rum.
3. Add .5 oz of Triple Sec.
4. Add .5 oz of White Crème De Menthe.
5. Add .5 oz of Lime Juice.
6. Add a dash of sugar syrup or .25 tsp of sugar.
7. Shake and strain into a chilled cocktail glass

Sax Rohmer

11
The Gin and Tonic
A Simple Solution To A Dangerous Problem

British soldiers from the British East India Company suffered from malaria while in the tropical heat of India. They were given tonic water to fight off the malaria because tonic water contained high levels of quinine, the active ingredient needed to fend off the disease. The problem was, quinine tastes terrible. Luckily soldiers received a daily ration of gin that they added to the tonic water in order to make it drinkable. Over time, these men acquired a taste for the combination and when they got home, they continued to order it at their favorite pubs.

The drink is still popular today although today's tonic water doesn't contain enough quinine to fend off the disease, something you should beware of if you ever find yourself fighting an enemy in a malaria-infested jungle.

The Classic Gin and Tonic
1. Add 3 oz of Gin to a chilled Highball Glass
2. Add 4 or 5 ice cubes made from Tonic Water.
3. Add 4 oz of Tonic Water.
4. Add 1 tablespoon of freshly squeezed Lime Juice.
5. Stir and garnish with a Lime Wedge.

There are as many kinds of the Gin and Tonic as there are ingredients you can add: variations include everything from cucumbers, to strawberries, to blueberry jam.

12
Cuba Libre
A Bar In Old Havana, Cuba, Circa 1900

A group of Teddy Roosevelt's Rough Riders are celebrating the defeat of Spain in the Spanish American War. The men are all wearing uniform shirts with button-down patch pockets open at the neck with blue bandanas. Suspenders hold up their khaki-colored pants while wide brown leather belts hold their sidearm holsters. Their boots are covered with leather spats up to the knees.

Captain Russel, an officer in the U.S. Signal Corp, approaches the bar and orders a new mixture of Bacardi Gold Rum, Coca-Cola, and a wedge of lime. Coca-Cola had just recently been introduced to Cuba. The new drink still had an exotic air surrounding it, not in small part due to the impact of an amount of cocaine included in the ingredients.

Captain Russel is so pleased with his new liquid creation that he orders a round of drinks for his fellow soldiers. The new mixture is a hit with the men. As they continue to drink, the ingredients start to take effect.

The men become boisterous, celebrating their recent victory over the Spanish. One soldier climbs up on his chair with the new drink in hand and announces, "Gentlemen, a toast to our victory, a toast to the newly freed Cuba. *Por Cuba Libre!* For Free Cuba!"

The celebrations continue with the men all shouting *Cuba Libre*... and so the Rum and Coke, or Cuba Libre, was born.

Was it really Captain Russel who came up with this combination of flavours; does it really matter? What matters is it tastes good even today, even without the extra pop the original cocaine provided. Talk about your Classic Coke, now that would be a taste test some people might want to check out.

John Pemberton

13
Coca-Cola and the Vin Mariani

I would be amiss if I didn't mention an additional word or two about the original version of Coca-Cola created by chemist John Stith Pemberton. Pemberton was a Lieutenant Colonel in the Confederate Army's Third Georgia Cavalry. He was wounded in battle and like many of his colleagues he became addicted to the morphine used as a painkiller. Being a pharmacist he experimented with finding an opium-free cure for his addiction. His initial attempts resulted in something called, *Dr. Tuggle's Compound Syrup of Globe Flower*, but he kept experimenting, no doubt concerned about how such a long brand name could ever fit on a bottle.

A Corsican chemist by the name of Angelo Mariani had already come up with what he called Vin Mariani, a combination of Bordeaux and cocaine that provided a generous energy boost. Using the Vin Mariani as inspiration, Pemberton came up with what he called *Pemberton's French Wine Coca*, by adding kola nut and damiana ingredients to Mariani's creation. Alcoholism and drug addiction were becoming an increasing problem among wounded war veterans like Pemberton; and according to ads for Pemberton's medicine, manic-depressive Southern Belles. In 1886 Fulton County, Atlanta, passed temperance legislation forcing Pemberton to find a substitute for the alcohol content. Pemberton worked with chemist Willis Venable and marketing maven Frank Mason Robinson to find a suitable solution. The result was Coca-Cola. Unfortunately for Pemberton, nothing he invented cured his dependence on morphine. His costly addiction eventually forced him to sell his share in the business. In 1888, shortly after the sale he died.

The Cuba Libre

The Cuba Libre gained further marketing attention with the popularity of *The Andrew Sisters* catchy WWII song, *Rum and Coca-Cola*. The war-time success of the Cuba Libre was helped along by The Coca-Cola Company's ability to get supplied with the sugar needed to make the product, an advantage other competitors were unable to match.

How To Make A Cuba Libre

1. Squeeze half a Lime into a Highball Glass.
2. Add 2 or 3 ice cubes.
3. Add 2 oz of Light Rum.
4. Fill with Coca-Cola.
5. Add the remains of the Lime.
6. Stir and serve.

How To Make An El Presidente

If you thought we exhausted the inventive beverage creation power of Cuba, think again. In addition to the Mojito, Daiquiri, and Cuba Libre, Cuba is responsible for the El Presidente, a popular drink during prohibition named in honor of Cuban President Mario Garcia Menocal.

1. Add 1.5 oz of White Rum to a shaker.
2. Add .75 oz of Orange Curacao.
3. Add .75 oz of Dry Vermouth.
4. Add 1 dash of Grenadine.
5. Fill with ice.
6. Shake well.
7. Strain into a chilled Cocktail Glass.
8. Garnish with an Orange Peel Twist.

H. E. Rasske

14
Monkey Business
The Legend of a Master Spy

A man in his early forties smoking a cigarette stands across the street from the Brass Monkey Lounge in the Portuguese colony of Macao. The year is 1942 and despite being neutral, the war in the Pacific rages all around the tiny island oasis, a haven for all sorts of scoundrels, rogues, and villains.

Macao is a bizarre blend of Portuguese Mediterranean-inspired architecture blended with an odd mix of Chinese culture and artefact. The man, H.E. Rasske, takes one last drag from his cigarette as he carefully eyes the comings and goings across the Street of Many Promises. His specific interest is the weird life-sized brass monkey that dominates the façade and guards the arched-door entrance of the Brass Monkey Lounge.

As far as anyone knows, Rasske is an Austrian businessman specializing in import-export. In fact, he is an American spy working to disrupt the Japanese war effort by supplying guns to the Chinese through a series of less than respectable *dhow* captains, river pirates, and mercenaries. Rasske tosses the remains of his cigarette into the gutter, brushes ash off his stylish European-cut tropical suit, and crosses the street dodging several rickshaws pulled by men in baggy pants and *dǒulì* hats.

He enters the Brass Monkey carefully eyeing the eclectic mix of Portuguese architecture and Chinese kitsch. He finds a stool at the bar and scans the surrounding balcony and tables all occupied by an assortment of Chinese bouncers, drunken sailors, and dissipated expatriates on the make. He signals the bartender and orders the house specialty, a sunshine yellow mixture of vodka, rum, Galliano, and orange juice.

A tough looking *dhow* captain takes the stool beside Rasske, waves to the bartender, and points to what Rasske is drinking. "I'll have one of those," he says. Neither man talks nor even acknowledges the other. The bartender delivers the drink and places it on a coaster printed with "The Brass Monkey" above an image of the brass statue that guards the bar.

The *dhow* captain takes a sip from his drink and starts doodling on the coaster with a pen he's taken from his work shirt pocket. When the captain is finished scribbling, he puts the coaster down so that Rasske has a perfect view. Written on the coaster are the words "No Evil". On further inspection Rasske sees the letters that spell out "See, Hear, and Speak" have been crossed out, what remains are the letters that spell "H.E. Rasske."

Rasske stands to leave and as he gets off the barstool, he casually bumps into the captain thereby getting close enough to slip a note into the sailor's jacket pocket. The *dhow* captain picks up the coaster and slips it into his shirt pocket. He waits several minutes allowing Rasske time to disappear down the street. The sailor finishes his drink and heads back to the docks.
Later that night the captain waits near his *dhow* smoking a cigarette. Out from the shadows of shipping containers steps H. E. Rasske. He stands half in the glow of a lantern so the

captain can see him. They meet, exchange some words, and within a few minutes Rasske has disappeared back into the shadows. The result of the meeting is another shipment of guns delivered to the Chinese forces fighting the Imperial Japanese.

The drink ordered by Rasske became known as the Brass Monkey cocktail, the drink that helped defeat the Japanese by fooling Admiral Kokura's Secret Service tasked with stopping arms shipments to the Chinese.

After the War Rasske retired to the Midwest and spent his days tending the roses in his garden and playing with his grandchildren, or at least that's the story told by advertising executives Steve Doniger and Allan Kaufman who came up with the whole elaborate tale in an effort to promote the sales of Heublein's Brass Monkey spirit cocktail.

Ads describing the adventures of master spy H.E. Rasske appeared in various magazines and newspapers around 1972. The drink gained more recognition after the release of the 1980s Beastie Boys rap single called Brass Monkey.

The Bass Monkey

How To Make A Brass Monkey
There are several variations of the Brass Monkey including a premixed cocktail sold under *The Club Cocktails* brand name owned by Diageo.

How To Make A Brass Monkey
1. Add 1 oz White Rum to a shaker.

2. Add 1 oz Vodka.
3. Add 2.5 oz of freshly squeezed Lemon Juice.
4. Add 1 oz Sugar Syrup (2 sugar to 1 water).
5. Add ice, shake, and strain into ice-filled Highball glass.
6. Garnish with a Lemon Slice.

An Alternative Variation
1. Fill an Old Fashion Glass with ice.
2. Add .5 oz of Light Rum.
3. Add .5 oz of Vodka.
4. 4 oz of Orange Juice
5. Stir well.
6. Add .5 oz of Galliano poured over the back of a spoon so it sits on top.

Freezing The Balls Off A Brass Monkey

Now you might be asking yourself how did they come up with the expression, "cold enough to freeze the balls off a brass monkey"? And the answer has nothing to do with cocktails, spies, or advertising campaigns, but it might make for an interesting discussion over a couple of cocktails named after the big brass simian.

On early sailing war ships the cannonballs would be stacked in a pyramid in order to store them. In order to keep the cannonballs from rolling around the gun deck every time the ship was hit by a big wave, small brass plates with rounded indentations, called brass monkeys, were positioned on the lowest level of the pyramid keeping the cannonballs from scattering.

Brass was used so it wouldn't rust to the iron cannonballs, but brass contracts in the cold. If it got cold enough, the rounded portions of the brass monkeys would shrink, causing the cannonballs to pop out, creating havoc on the gun deck, hence the expression, "cold enough to freeze the balls off a brass monkey."

And of course the United States Navy Historical Center says this explanation is a made-up legend taken from the book "Before the Mast" by C. A. Abbey. It seems you just can't believe anything anyone tells you.

Serge Voronoff

15
The Monkey Gland

Speaking of freezing the balls off a brass monkey brings us to another exotic libation that calls forth the restorative healing power of our ape cousins. Of all the monkey-inspired cocktails the one with the most interesting documented history is the Monkey Gland, so named by famous bartender Harry MacElhone, the Scottish borne owner of Harry's New York Bar in Paris, France.

Harry was responsible for inventing a number of famous cocktails including, the Bloody Mary, the Sidecar, and the White Lady. And then of course, there's the Monkey Gland created in the 1920s by Harry to celebrate the fascinating and bizarre tale of surgical experimentation.

Serge Voronoff was a French surgeon born in a Russian village in the summer of 1866. He immigrated to France and studied medicine, becoming a surgeon. Although Voronoff was independently wealthy, he gained further fame and fortune for his experiments in grafting monkey testicle tissue onto testosterone-challenged men throughout the 1920s and 30s.

Lest you think Voronoff was a complete quack it should be noted that he studied transplantation techniques under Nobel Prize winner Alexis Carrel. From 1896 to 1910 he spent time in Egypt studying the effects of castration on eunuchs in an effort to reverse the effects. In an experiment in 1889 designed to retard the effects of aging he actually injected himself with ground-up dog and guinea pig testicles, now that's what I call commitment. The procedure failed leading Voronoff to conclude that glandular transplantation would be a better course of treatment.

Some of his early efforts included transplanting chimpanzee thyroid glands into humans in order to combat thyroid deficiencies. Here's where it gets a little weird or perhaps weirder. His next batch of mad scientist, *Frankensteinian* antics involved transplanting the tissue from the testicles of executed criminals to eager elderly millionaires in an effort to stiffen their resolve.

Unfortunately the demand from wealthy horny old men outstripped the supply of death row inmates. In 1923 at the International Congress of Surgeons in London, England, Voronoff was lauded for his groundbreaking work on the "rejuvenation" of old men. It was meant to be the Viagra of the 1920s: a solution for men who weren't hard up. Voronoff actually believed his techniques not only improved sex drive, but memory, stamina, and even eyesight.

As you can imagine, the demand for this magical medical fixer upper was substantial, a fact that must have sent the monkey population running for their lives while grasping tightly to their crown jewels. Ashtrays made of monkeys protecting their testicles began popping up all over the parlours of Paris. To keep up with the demand, not for the ashtrays but for the monkey parts, Voronoff created a monkey farm on the Italian Riviera run by an ex-circus animal wrangler. You can just imagine what PETA would have done with that bit of news.

And so that brings us to Harry MacElhone, proprietor and chief mixologist at Harry's New York Bar in Paris, France. Never one to let a good opportunity to promote the bar go by, Harry came up with his Monkey Gland mixture of gin, orange juice, absinthe, and Grenadine, a sure cure for any customer looking for a quick pick-me-up.

Alas poor Voronoff's methods eventually fell out of favor and his invasive techniques were dismissed as no more effective than a placebo. He died in obscurity in 1951 with barely a mention in the press, however Harry's cocktail lives on as a reminder of man's desire for everlasting virility, and his love of a potent gin thirst quencher.

Monkey Related Drinks
Monkey Gland, Funky Monkey, and Cheeky Monkey

How To Make A Monkey Gland
1. Add 1.5 oz of Gin to a shaker with ice.
2. Add 1.5 oz of Orange Juice.
3. Add 1 tsp of Absinthe
4. Add 1 tsp of Grenadine.
5. Shake and strain into chilled Cocktail Glass.

How To Make A Funky Monkey
1. Add 1 oz of White Rum to a Highball Glass.
2. Add 1 oz of Banana Liqueur.
3. Add .5 oz of Coconut Rum.
4. Fill with Pineapple Juice.
5. Stir and add crushed ice.
6. Garnish with two Maraschino Cherries.

How To Make A Cheeky Monkey
1. Fill a shaker with ice cubes.
2. Add 2 oz of Absolut Citron Vodka.
3. Add 4 oz of Orange Juice.
4. Add 2 oz of Yellow Chartreuse.
5. Add oz of Simple Syrup.
6. Add 4 dashes of Orange Bitters.
7. Shake and strain into a chilled Cocktail Glass.

Wing Commander Montgomery Collins

16
Monkey 47

Thought we were finished with monkeys, well not just yet. I confess, this is not a cocktail, but it is the name of a famous, unusual gin that goes by the name of Monkey 47, and comes from a place more well known for its ham and beer than it does for its gin.

But let's start at the beginning with Wing Commander Montgomery "Monty" Collins of the Royal Air Force. Monty was born in 1909, the son of a British Diplomat in British-controlled India in the province of Madras. Monty loved watches and was a whiz at languages, eventually able to speak five, including German. His love of watches and the German language may seem irrelevant now, but they do play a part in the story of Monkey 47.

After WWII Berlin was divided into four sectors each controlled by one of the allies: the United States, Britain, France, and the Soviet Union. Monty was posted to the British Sector of Berlin. The city had been almost completely destroyed by allied bombing and Soviet shelling. Monty wanted to help in the reconstruction in some small way, so in his spare time he volunteered with the rebuilding of the Berlin Zoo. His efforts included sponsoring an egret monkey named Max.

In 1951 Monty retired to a village in the Northern Black Forest in order to learn watch making, but watch making was not in

Monty's wheelhouse, so instead he opened a country guesthouse that he called *Zum Wilden Affen*, or The Wild Monkey, in honor of his adopted primate friend Max. Searching for something to do, Monty started looking around the local region and discovered there was a plentiful supply of Juniper used in the production of Black Forest Ham, crystal clear well water, and a great variety of herbs and plants; all ingredients that could be used in the production of gin.

Sometime in the early 1960s the story of Commander Montgomery Collins fades to gray. You'll notice I said gray not black, because around the turn of the century, while working on renovating the *Zum Wilden Affen*, workers discovered a large heavy chest containing numerous Collins artefacts and memorabilia. Included among the items was a dusty bottle with a hand drawn label featuring a monkey surrounded by the words, "*Max The Monkey*" on the top and "*Schwarzwald Dry Gin*" on the bottom. Also included in the chest were notes detailing how Monty dreamt one night of the recipe for his Black Forest Gin as well as a list of ingredients and instructions on how to make it.

So you ask, where does the 47 come into the picture? It seems Monty's recipe calls for forty-seven different ingredients. Of course as pointed out in The Monkey Drum blog on the monkey47.com website, forty-seven is also the number of words in the Hawaiian language for bananas, and we all know what animal likes bananas.

Monkeys Gone Bad

Now this whole monkey business seems all cute and cuddly because really who doesn't like monkeys? Well as it turns out the people of India aren't too fond of the little creatures. In fact according to David Whelan's report, *"India Is Being Overtaken by Armies of Defiant Monkeys"* published on the vice.com website, monkeys in India have become a downright nuisance. Yeah, yeah, I know this has nothing to do with how cocktails got their names, but work with me here it's interesting.

According to the article there are fifty million monkeys overrunning India, and the little buggers seem intent on taking over the cities. I suppose you can't blame them, after all the cities are taking over their territories. The monkeys raid peoples' homes and steal their food; sometimes they get into some homemade hooch. Believe it or not, drunken monkeys have been seen stumbling around in a Harvey Wallbanger kind of haze.

They raid the food stalls of the poor souls just trying to eke out a living in the marketplace with coordinated tactical assaults, and they are relentless. Peddlers try to chase them off with sticks but at the same time they are revered and protected by the Hindu Monkey God Hanuman, and so there isn't much ordinary people can do.

This may sound humorous but the problem has become serious and occasionally deadly. The Deputy Mayor of Delhi, S.S. Bajwa was pushed off his balcony by a horde of crazed monkeys. And according to the Vice article there are eleven thousand political documents that have disappeared from the Home Ministry, and apparently some people swear they've seen monkeys scampering down the halls of government buildings carrying stolen political documents.

If Monty would have known the problem monkeys would be causing in the place of his birth, he might have chosen another animal to sponsor, but then you might be stuck with Wild Ass 47 instead of Monkey 47.

17
Drunken Monkey

Speaking of drunken monkeys, there just happens to be a cocktail called the Drunken Monkey. This potent, deceivingly benign mixture of alcohol is the brainchild of Mike Lenk. It seems that Mike was at a party were Flaming Hot Pumpkin Pies were the hot beverage du jour, and when I say hot, I do mean hot, because the Flaming Hot Pumpkin Pie is one of those drinks that can set your house on fire. Mike must have been a little concerned about the dangers of a bunch of drunken pyromaniacs, so he came up with a delightful combination that was strong but safe.

Mike had been recently introduced to a ninety-ninety proof banana schnapps, appropriately named 99 Bananas, but unlike its fruit namesake, too many of these babies and you might just turn into one of those crazed drunken simians that attack Indian government officials and steal their documents.

By the way, have you ever wondered why alcohol content is measured in *proof*? Back in the good old days, British sailors were given a daily ration of rum. Seamen being cynical sorts figured the authorities watered down the rum, either to stretch the inventory so it went further, or to guard against inebriated seaman falling overboard. To test the rum to see if it was of appropriate strength, sailors would add gunpowder and try to set it on fire. It really does seem that people are always trying to set their drinks on fire, doesn't it?

In any case, if the rum and gunpowder mixture was able to produce flames, it was *proof* that the rum was of appropriate potency. The practice of allowing seamen a daily ration of, originally beer, then rum, was started in the 1600s but was finally halted on July 31, 1970 on what sailors call Black Tot Day.

Back to Mike Lent and his creation. It seems Mike had a pet wooden monkey, The Monkey With A Fez, and of course the monkey was a great Cleveland Browns' football fan. It sounds crazy I know, you'd think any wooden monkey who knows anything about football would be more of a New England Patriots' fan, but then what do I know, Canadian football only has three downs, go figure.

According to Mike it was the monkey that suggested using the 99 Bananas as a shot, but after a sample or two, Mike felt the banana flavor was a bit overwhelming. The drink needed something added to tone down the strong banana taste, so he added some Bailey's Irish Cream and some Kahlúa Coffee Liqueur. The newly minted Drunken Monkey was a hit whenever Mike introduced it to partygoers.

It should be pointed out that although the Drunken Monkey tastes like a deliciously sweet milkshake, it is one potent cocktail that comes in at 68 proof.

How To Make A Drunken Monkey
1. Fill a shaker with ice cubes.
2. Add 1 oz of 99 Bananas banana schnapps.
3. Add .5 oz of Bailey's Irish Cream.
4. Add .5 oz of Kahlua coffee liqueur.
5. Shake and pour into a Martini Glass.

Marjorie King

18
The Margarita Mystery

Like most cocktails the Margarita's origin is steeped in mystery and competing versions of who and where it was invented. Any number of beautiful or at least quasi-famous Margarita's have insisted that they are the quintessential Margarita in question. Although the Margarita's tequila base gives the cocktail it's Mexican pedigree, most mixologist historians would argue that mixed drinks are not a Mexican thing, and so a Mexican-American heritage is the most likely creation-scenario, although there may be a German association as well. And of course there's the Daisy connection that can't be ignored; but as the French say, or at least what Hollywood says the French say, "*cherchez la femme,*" find the woman.

Marjorie King
Margarita Contender No.1

Femme fatale number one is sometime actress and showgirl Marjorie King. A search for Marjorie King produces a beautiful black-and-white photograph of a nude woman coyly positioned in profile, her head tucked into her chin, her eyes closed, looking down, her arms are pressed close to her body covering her breasts, her legs are crossed with a sheer black fabric draped over her knees. All she's wearing is a long string of pearls draped over the crook of her arm and dark high heel shoes. Her hair is jet-black cut in a stylish short-cropped 1920s wavy style, which is not surprising since Marjorie King was a

Ziegfeld showgirl and B-celebrity actress. The photograph shows everything and nothing; what it does reveal is that she was a beauty, and perhaps the perfect inspiration for the cocktail we call the Margarita.

One Carlos Danny Herrera claims title to creator of the Marjorie King Margarita. Herrera lived in Baja, California and was owner of the Rancho La Gloria resort, a small but popular watering hole favored by celebrities and their playmates on their way to Rosarita Beach. According to Herrera, Marjorie and her friends stopped off for some rest, relaxation, and refreshments. Everyone was drinking and having a good time, everyone except the prickly beauty who explained to Danny that she was allergic to all alcohol except tequila but unfortunately she didn't like the taste.

Danny being the perfect host and an inventive bartender, not to mention a brilliant promoter, started to experiment searching for the perfect mix of ingredients to please a woman use to being satisfied. The result, as legend has it, is the Margarita, a combination of tequila, Cointreau, and lemon juice, a combination that the hard to please beauty found to her liking. Not being one to let a major marketing opportunity go by without fanfare, Danny dubbed the new creation the Margarita. And why not the Marjorie you ask? Well Danny being Mexican chose the Spanish equivalent of Marjorie as the name, and so the Margarita was borne.

Margaret Sames

19
Margaret Sames
Contender No.2

Femme fatale number two is Margaret Sames, a thirty-five-year-old socialite from Dallas. According to Sames she is the creator of the Margarita. In 1948, Sames and her husband Bill rented a house in Acapulco while their own luxury hacienda was being built. To celebrate Christmas, the Sames invited a few friends to join them: Nicky Hilton, hotel czar, Shelton McHenry, owner of the Tail O' the Cock, Joseph Drown, Hotel Bel-Air proprietor, and movie stars Lana Turner and John Wayne. Just your average socialite holiday get together.

Of course you can't invite a slew of big name celebrities without offering them something more than your run-of-the-mill luxury Acapulco vacation retreat. Sames decided that the party wouldn't be complete without offering her guests a delicious new alcoholic concoction of her own design. Interviewed in 1994 by the *San Antonio News-Express*, Mrs. Sames is quoted as saying, "After all, a person can only drink so many beers or so many Bloody Marys, or Screwdrivers, or whatever. I wanted to make up a new drink." If nothing else, Mrs. Sames knew how to promote herself.

As she tells it, she initially tried rum as her alcohol base, a taste she acquired on her vacations to Cuba. It seems socialites take a lot of vacations. In any case, it didn't work, so she moved on to her favorite, tequila, a logical choice since she was partying in

Mexico. Since she had also acquired a taste for Cointreau, she decided to mix the French liqueur with Mexican tequila. Her attempts were greeted with a less than enthusiastic reception. The failure resulted in her guinea pig guests tossing her into the pool.

Her experiments were either too sweet or too acerbic until she added lime juice to even out the flavours. The result was a success. Margarita's Drink, as it was dubbed by her guests, became the cocktail of choice whenever Bill and Margarita Sames threw one of their celebrity soirees. The new cocktail became a Sames tradition, with Bill celebrating his wife's creation by presenting her with a set of glasses etched with her name on them.

Celebrity hotel magnate, Nicky Hilton put the newly invented cocktail on the bar menu at all his hotels. Other celebrity friends, who were either Hollywood royalty, or nightclub owners, spread the word about Margarita's Drink, at least that's the story Margarita Sames told the *San Antonio News-Express*.

20
Margarita Henkel
Contender No.3

Femme fatale number three is Margarita Henkel. The story of her claim to the Margarita could start with the line, *"a girl walks into a Mexican bar."* Henkel was the daughter of the German Ambassador to Mexico prior to Mexico declaring war on Germany for sinking two Mexican oil tankers. The ships were delivering crude to the United States during the Second World War. Mexico and Brazil were the only two Latin American countries that joined the allies in the fight against the axis powers.

Don Carlos Orozco says he's the guy who invented the Margarita in honor of the Ambassador's daughter who just happened to wander into Ussong's Cantina in Ensenada, Mexico. But before we get to Don Carlos and Margarita Henkel, we must first go back to the beginning of this tale because the preamble is a lot more interesting than the arguable claims of bartender Don Carlos Orozco.

Johann, John, Hussong was born in Forsham Germany in 1863. He immigrated to the United States in 1888 and then on to Ensenada in 1889 where gold was discovered. Hussong made a living hunting and trading up and down the Baja coast selling to local restaurants. In 1890 he bought a barbershop and started a carriage line between Ensenada and the gold rush camps in El

Alamo. This is where the story gets a little blurry. While on one of his trips his wagon flipped over and either he or his companion, Newt House, broke their leg. Hussong went to Ensenada so either he or his friend could recuperate at the towns only bar, the J. J. Meiggs' Cantina.

A few days after their arrival, Meiggs attacked his wife with an axe. Why? Nobody knows. Meiggs was put in jail and his wife skedaddled to California. For some reason they let Meiggs out of jail, presumably the crime of attempted murder was no big deal back then if your intended victim was only your wife. In any case, Meiggs took off after his wife motivated by either a sincere desire to apologize, or perhaps to finish the job. Before he left, Meiggs asked Hussong to look after the bar for him while he was away. Again there are those that say Meiggs sold it to Hussong. In any case, Meiggs and his wife were never seen, or heard from, ever again.

Hussong ran the bar for a year and presumably liked the work. He understood the town had potential, based on the fact it was the end of the line for steamships that ran between San Diego and Ensenada. Hussong bought the building across the street from Meiggs and remodelled it creating Hussong's Cantina. In 1892 he applied for and received Ensenada's second liquor license #002. Hussong's Cantina is still located in the same building on Ruiz Avenue, and from what we're told it hasn't changed very much. It's still owned by Hussong's grandson, Ricardo.

Because the bar was strategically located at the end of the line and because it was the only bar in town, it became a hangout for movie stars like Bing Crosby, Ronald Reagan, Marilyn Monroe, Humphrey Bogart, and John Wayne, one of Margaret Sames Christmas Party guests. One assumes that celebrities found the isolation to their liking. Being away from the Hollywood paparazzi-infested fish bowl, allowed them to play without worry of being spotted.

Since the frontier bar seemed to have become a celebrity hotspot of sorts, it's not surprising Margarita Henkel, daughter of the German Ambassador, found her way through the front door. And according to Don Carlos Orozco, he was so impressed with the ambassador's daughter, he named the tequila, Damiana (Controy), and lime mixture the Margarita in her honor, since she was the first to try it. Okay, I know what you're thinking, Marilyn Monroe was a regular, but he named his creation after Henkel? You make up your own mind.

Margarita Cansino (Rita Hayworth)

21
Margarita Cansino
Contender No.4

Femme fatale number four is Margarita Cansino. Bartender Danny Negrete claims he is the inventor of the popular tequila, Cointreau, and limejuice cocktail. Negrete claims he invented the drink at the Garci Crespo Hotel as a wedding present for his sister-in-law, Margarita. Doesn't really sound like much of a wedding present if you ask me, but what is interesting is that Negrete worked at the Agua Cliente Race Track where a teenage Margarita Cansino performed as a dancer with her abusive father. Cansino's father pushed his teenage daughter into more and more provocative costumes and dances.

He often referred to her as his wife and not his daughter. His abusive behavior scarred his daughter's life and her relationship with men, despite going on to become a major motion picture star and sex symbol. Despite Negrete's claim of creating the Margarita for his sister-in-law, there are those that believe he actually named it after the beautiful, sexy dancer he saw perform at the Aqua Cliente Race Track.

According to Barbara Leaming's biography of Cansino, *If This Was Happiness*, the beautiful dark-haired sixteen-year-old appeared in a Spencer Tracy movie, *Dante's Inferno* performing what was considered in those days to be a rather daring dance routine. The studio press release marketing the movie referred to Cansino as Rita rather than the more accurate Margarita. A couple of years later she married a sleazy character named Eddie Johnson who saw the sensuous teenager as his meal ticket. In what was to become a hackneyed Hollywood cliché Johnson remade his young wife into a gorgeous red-haired sex symbol featured in many movies and gracing the pages of numerous movie magazines, including one famous Bob Landry photograph that appeared in *Life* magazine.

Unlike the other women who claim to be the inspiration for the Margarita, Casino would become known for much more than just a tequila cocktail. You might recognize Margarita Cansino better as Rita Hayworth.

22
Margarita Mendes
Contender No. 5

Femme fatale number five is Margarita Mendes, a hot-tempered beauty and the girlfriend of bartender Red Hinton. Hinton claims he invented the Margarita in his girlfriend's memory. His version of the Margarita used tequila and a mixture of lemon and orange juice presented in a salted glass. Decide for yourself the veracity of his claim.

Picture if you will the dusty frontier town of Virginia City, Nevada. The place looks like something out of an old episode of *Gunsmoke*. Yes, I know *Gunsmoke* took place in Dodge City but work with me. You'd almost expect to see Kitty's girls hanging out on the balcony of the building beside the Crystal Bar, with Chester, Doc, and Matt Dillon leaning back on their wooden chairs keeping out of the scorching midday sun.

According to legend, Mendes had a bit of a temper, and for some reason decided to hit some guy over the head with a bottle of whiskey. This seemed to upset Robert Arthur who was a friend of the fellow Mendes attacked, and besides, it seemed like a complete waste of a perfectly good bottle of whiskey.

Arthur drew his revolver and fired off a warning shot intended to scare Mendes. Unfortunately, the bullet hit her in the head killing her. Obviously Arthur didn't have very good aim. He was arrested, but soon freed, as the brilliantly chauvinistic law enforcement officials of Virginia City decided that if Arthur really wanted to kill Mendes, he would have shot at her chest and not her head. Go figure frontier justice. The heartbroken bartender, Red Hinton, claims to have memorialized his hot-tempered lover with a new tequila based cocktail named in her honor.

23
The Daisy
Contender No.6

Finally we get to Daisy, not a beautiful woman but rather a tasty liquid refreshment that dates back to the late eighteen hundreds. The classic recipe called for a base spirit of brandy, whiskey, or gin with simple syrup, Curacao or Maraschino, lemon juice, and soda water. This combination was to become the basis for several future cocktails with different names and histories.

During Prohibition alcohol was of course banned and the good stuff was hard to get. Celebrities and socialites found that escaping to foreign lands to party was a safe alternative to sneaking around in illegal speakeasies although that too had its cachet. In any case, Mexico was close to Hollywood and a perfect location for partying movie types to escape to for a little fun. Since Mexico wasn't a brandy kind of place, tequila was often substituted. When people wanted a Daisy with tequila, they would ask for a Margarita since Daisy in Spanish is Margarita.

The Margarita

How To Make A Margarita
1. Add ingredients to a shaker with ice.
2. Add 1.5 oz of Tequila (blanco, 100% agave).
3. Add 1 oz fresh of Lime Juice.
4. Add .5 oz of Cointreau
5. Shake and strain into Cocktail Glass
6. Fill glass halfway with ice
7. Rub the rim of glass with a Lime Slice
8. Salt the rim of the glass.
9. Garnish with a Lime Slice.

How To Make A Daisy
1. Add 1.5 oz of Brandy to shaker with cracked ice.
2. Add .75 oz of Yellow Chartreuse.
3. Add .75 oz of Lemon Juice.
4. Stir well and strain into chilled Collins Glass.
5. Top with a splash of chilled Club Soda or Seltzer.

24
The Tom Collins Hoax of 1874

Perhaps you can chalk this seemingly silly episode in cocktail history up to the lack of the Internet, movies, television, and radio. Obviously people didn't have enough appropriate options for entertaining themselves. Sure there were books to read but quietly reading a book lacks the alcoholic fuelled social intercourse that people crave.

After a few alcohol-induced hours of imbibing one's favorite liquid refreshment, it's easy to understand how conversations turned to social high jinks. It seems the people of the last quarter of the nineteenth century had a rather infantile understanding of humor although a brief perusal of the Internet and its various social media self-indulgences leads one to conclude that things really haven't changed much.

It seems that in 1874 people thought it was great fun to meet friends in a bar with, "Have you seen Tom Collins?" When people answered that they didn't know a Tom Collins and therefore wouldn't know him if they had seen him, the prankster would reply, "Well, he's at a bar around the corner and he's saying some very nasty things about you."

This would of course upset the target of the gag. The instigator would continue encouraging the victim to confront the Collins rascal and to take some measure of revenge. Off the poor fellow would go in search of the non-existent Tom Collins. This practical joke was considered great fun in 1874 and spread like wildfire in the same way today's Internet cat videos tend to proliferate like a bad case of some social disease.

Even the newspapers of the time got into the act by printing Tom Collins sightings. Angry, drunk, bar hopping dupes would run all over New York City looking for the slandering rascal Tom Collins. Bartenders figured the scam shouldn't go to financial waste, so when somebody barged into their bars demanding Tom Collins, they would unknowingly be ordering a gin, sugar, and lemon juice cocktail. Those wild and crazy bartenders of 1874, they sure loved their practical jokes.

But like most cocktail histories the Tom Collins has a bit more of a story to tell. Why did bartenders of the time use the gin and lemon juice mixture instead of something else? To get the answer we have to go back a little further in cocktail history. It seems there was an Irish political activist who died in 1798 during the Irish Rebellion and some people suggest the Tom Collins is named in his honor, except the fellow in question was Michael Collins not Tom, so much for that theory.

And then there is the Frank and Charles Sheridan poem about recounting the tale of John Collins, the bartender at Limmer's Old House, a London Mayfair hotel and coffee house. It seems John Collins invented a gin punch mixture that he named after himself. The recipe for the John Collins as featured in the 1869

Steward and Barkeeper's Manual calls for sugar, lemon, plain soda and a wine glass of Old Tom Gin. It's the use of Old Tom Gin that over time resulted in changing the John Collins into the Tom Collins.

The Tom Collins

The Tom Collins Connection

It's easy to understand how the New York bartenders of 1874 came up with the idea of serving this particular mixture of Old Tom Gin, lemon juice, and soda to anyone entering their bars looking for a Tom Collins.

How To Make A Tom Collins

1. Fill Collins glass about .75 full with cracked ice.
2. Add 2 oz of Gin.
3. Add 1 tsp superfine sugar.
4. Add .5 oz of Lemon Juice.
5. Fill with Club Soda mix well and serve.
6. Garnish with a large Lemon Wedge.

Cocktails of New York's Five Boroughs

If you're a native New Yorker intent on honouring your city, you don't have to have a Manhattan although the Manhattan is by far the best known of the cocktails named after the five boroughs

Lady Randolph Churchill

25
The Manhattan

Like most cocktails the legend of how the Manhattan got its name is shrouded in mystery or should I say more accurately, inaccuracy. The legend states a Dr. Iain Marshall created the cocktail at the Manhattan Club for Lady Randolph Churchill, Jennie Jerome the American-born mother of Sir Winston Churchill, who is said to have hosted a banquet honoring presidential candidate Samuel J. Tilden.

The drink was popular and henceforth people requested the Manhattan cocktail. It's an interesting story except for the fact that Lady Randolph was resting in Europe pregnant, and so the story is fictional. One of the interesting historical side-notes to Tilden's run for the Presidency is that he won the popular vote but lost the election by virtue of losing the electoral vote, giving the Presidency to Rutherford B. Hayes.

How To Make A Manhattan
1. Add 2 oz of Rye (or Bourbon) to mixing glass.
2. Add 1 oz of Sweet Vermouth.
3. Add 2 dashes of Aromatic (Angostura) Bitters.
4. Stir in 30 and strain into Cocktail Glass.
5. Garnish with a Maraschino Cherry.

26
The Bronx

The Bronx cocktail has been described as a Perfect Martini with the addition of orange juice. The Perfect Martini uses equal amounts of sweet and dry vermouth, as opposed to a Dry Martini that's made with dry, white vermouth, or a Dirty Martini that's made with a splash of olive brine or olive juice. Two people claim to be the inventor of the Bronx cocktail: Joseph S. Sormani and Johnnie Solon. Bronx restaurateur, Sormani claims he discovered the basic recipe in Philadelphia in 1905. The original recipe used four parts gin to one part orange juice and one part Italian Vermouth.

The Solon story is far more interesting. According to Albert Crockett, historian of the famous Waldorf-Astoria Hotel, Johnnie Solon, a Pre-Prohibition bartender at the Waldorf invented the drink for the headwaiter in the hotel's main dining room, a fellow named Traverson.

Traverson had a regular customer that was looking for something new and suggested Solon might just be the fellow to create it. At the time Solon was making what was called a Duplex, a cocktail made with French and Italian Vermouth, orange juice and orange bitters. The Duplex sparked his imagination and before Traverson knew it, Solon had invented the new drink. Traverson was excited after tasting the new cocktail and demanded Solon make one for his customer. Before he delivered the drink to his customer, he asked Solon what he should call it. Solon had just been to the Bronx Zoo where he saw animals he'd never seen before. The strange animals reminded him of the imagined wild beasts he'd heard patrons describe after enjoying one too many of his liquid creations. And so Solon suggested they call it the Bronx. The fact that the drink was technically not named after the borough, but after the zoo, shouldn't stop any Bronxite from claiming the cocktail as his or her own.

How To Make A Bronx Cocktail
1. Add 2 oz of Gin to shaker with ice.
2. Add .25 oz of Sweet Vermouth.
3. Add .25 oz of Dry Vermouth.
4. Add 1 oz fresh of Orange Juice.
3. Add Orange Bitters to your liking.
4. Shake and strain Cocktail Glass.
5. Garnish with an Orange Twist.

27
The Brooklyn Cocktail

This is the sad tale of the Brooklyn cocktail, the Rodney Dangerfield of mixed drinks, the concoction that couldn't get "no respect." It seems that the creation of the rival Manhattan and Bronx cocktails led to a severe case of cocktail-envy. Brooklyn was developing an alcohol inferiority complex; they had to develop their own signature drink. The Pre-Prohibition boroughs were separate towns at the time. Why should rival towns have drinks named in their honor and not the proud city of Brooklyn? And so the mixing began. Our search for the history of the Brooklyn cocktail led us to an article in *Edible Brooklyn* by David Wondrich who seems to have brought together all the facts available.

According to Wondrich, the initial Brooklyn cocktail created by Jacob Grohusko can be found in his 1908 mixing guide, *Jack's Manual*. The combination of rye whiskey, dry vermouth, maraschino liqueur, and Amer Picon made for an acceptable signature drink. Unfortunately it didn't capture anyone's imagination including the citizens of Brooklyn.

In 1910 a lawyer named Henry Wellington Wack created his version by adding a spoon of raspberry syrup to gin and equal parts sweet and dry vermouth. The effort was greeted with a less than enthusiastic response. The fact it was nothing more than a Perfect Martini with fruit syrup didn't help. What's interesting, or not, is none of the inventors lived in Brooklyn, perhaps that would have added some sense of authenticity to the exercise.

Yet another attempt in 1910 combined absinthe, hard cider, and ginger ale, but that too was met with apathy. In 1913 Grohusko's Brooklyn was included in Jacques Straub's *Manual of Mixed Drinks*, a popular source of mixology, but again it was greeted with silence. Despite the apathy, Grohusko's Brooklyn was gaining respect and was included in both the *Savoy Cocktail Book* and the *Official Mixer's Manual*, but popularity remained elusive.

In 1934 another attempt by Brad Dewey of the Gage & Tollner, a respected Brooklyn eatery, was anointed the Brooklyn. According to Wondrich it was either a combination of gin, grapefruit and grenadine, or Jamaican rum, lime juice, and grenadine. Again, nobody cared. Grohusko's version still survives in small pockets of nostalgia as the default signature Brooklyn. Perhaps the cocktail that gets no respect is a fitting representative for the borough that is best remembered as the place even a baseball team abandoned.

Grohusko's Brooklyn
The retelling of the sad Brooklyn cocktail saga highlights the fact that the crazy concoctions that manage to survive and gain popularity are truly innovations that deserve some measure of respect if not for taste then at least for marketing.

How To Make A Brooklyn Cocktail
1. Add 2 oz of Rye/Blended Whiskey to shaker with ice.
2. Add 1 oz of Dry Vermouth
3. Add a dash of Maraschino Liqueur
4. Add a dash of Amer Picon (or Torani Amer).
5. Shake and strain Cocktail Glass.

28
The Queens Cocktail

If all the other future boroughs of New York City were going to have cocktails named in their honor, then Queens needed one as well. In 1930 Harry Craddock's *Savoy Cocktail Book* lists the

Queens Cocktail as a variation of the Perfect Martini with pineapple juice added.

How To Make A Queens Cocktail
1. Add 1 oz of Gin to shaker with ice.
2. Add 1 oz of Sweet Vermouth.
3. Add 1 oz of Dry Vermouth.
4. Add 1 oz of Pineapple Juice.
5. Shake and strain cocktail glass.

29
The Staten Island Cocktail

Staten Island was not going to standby while all its rival boroughs branded their very own signature drinks without responding in kind. Staten Island may not be a Caribbean paradise but their namesake drink could evoke the pleasures of relaxing in the tropics. To that end, their mixture of Malibu Rum and pineapple juice seemed an appropriate solution: not quite a Pina Colada, for an island, that was not quite Jamaica.

How To Make A Staten Island Cocktail
1. Add 2 oz of Malibu Rum to a mixing glass.
2. Add 2 oz of Pineapple Juice.
4. Fill a Highball Glass 2/3s with ice.
5. Pour the rum and Pineapple Juice into glass.

30
The Harvey Wallbanger

The legend of the Harvey Wallbanger is as muddled as the effect the drink produces after overindulging in the refreshment. In the 1950s a surfer named Harvey enjoyed a nightly cocktail or six of his own design after a hard day surfing. What he ordered was a Screwdriver, a simple vodka and orange juice combination but with the added touch of Galliano poured on top. After several of his potent creations Harvey was unable to navigate his way to the men's room without banging into several walls. The ritual of his nightly stumbling became so frequent that the drink he created was soon dubbed the Harvey Wallbanger.

Of course there's always someone willing to spoil a good legend with a more plausible explanation of how the Wallbanger was christened. Some say the cocktail was invented by Donato Duke Antone, a champion mixologist in 1952, and promoted by George Bednar in a sales campaign for Galliano in California. According to Antone's obituary in the *Hartford Courant*, Antone "created more than 50 drinks, including the famous Harvey Wallbanger, the Rusty Nail, the Flaming Caeser, the Duke Cocktail and the Italian Fascination."

What is even more interesting is the fact that Donato Duke Antone was a genuine WWII war hero and the recipient of two silver stars, two bronze stars, two Purple Hearts and a Croix de Guerre. Even if Antone was the true inventor of the Wallbanger that doesn't explain the name.

Perhaps the story is a myth or perhaps both stories are true. According to an article in *Saveur* by Robert Simonson, Antone could have invented the drink in 1952 and named it after a Manhattan

Beach surfer by the name of Tom Harvey. Both stories can be tied together in a plausible explanation, except for the fact that George Bednar head of marketing for McKesson Imports Co. might have created the whole thing as a marketing gimmick to promote the sale of Galliano.

The Harvey Wallbanger

The base upon which the Harvey Wallbanger is built is the Screwdriver, another drink with legendary beginnings. Although there are references to a Smirnoff Screwdriver as early as 1938, a story in *Time* magazine in 1949 referred to Turkish intelligence agents and American engineers partaking of the new cocktail.

It seems the vodka and orange juice combination was a favorite among the American oil workers, but these oilmen went out into the field without spoons, so instead, used screwdrivers to mix their drinks. What I find interesting is these guys forgot to take eating utensils but not the booze.

How To Make A Harvey Wallbanger
1. Add 1.5 oz of Vodka to Highball Glass with ice.
2. Add 3 oz of fresh Orange Juice and stir.
4. Float .5 oz of Galliano on top.
5. Garnish with a Maraschino Cherry and Orange Slice.

Toulouse Lautrec

31
The Earthquake and The Artist

A café in Montmartre, Paris 1892, an aristocratic man with a bohemian flair sits at a round table drinking and sketching his fellow patrons and passersby. The man is a fixture at the café as well as the many other drinking establishments, brothels, and entertainment venues in the area. Seated, the man almost looks normal, he wears a butterfly collared shirt, an expensive cravat, a waistcoat, suit jacket, gray trousers, and a bowler style hat. He sports a full beard, a monocle, and a specially constructed cane of his own design able to hold several vials of absinthe, his favorite substance of depravation.

He enjoys a drink of his own creation, a *Tremblement de Terre*, an Earthquake, a potent combination of three parts absinthe, three parts cognac, and some ice. His creativity is not solely devoted to his alcoholism for this bizarre little man with the upper torso of an adult and the stunted legs of a child is a well-known artist, Henri Marie Raymond de Toulouse-Lautrec-Monfa, more commonly known as Henri de Toulouse-Lautrec, an aristocratic borne artist who has a reputation not only as a great painter and printmaker but also as an avant garde bohemian indulger of Montmartre's seedier exotic pleasures.

He is joined at the table by an extremely attractive redhead dressed in a black dress with a plunging neckline, black silk neck adornment, and an expression of deep sadness and depravity. She is a dancer at the Moulin Rouge, and one of Lautrec's favorite subjects. A waiter recognizing the famous dancer brings a bottle of absinthe, an odd-looking glass, a drip spoon, a jar of sugar cubes, and a carafe of ice water. In terms of sheer complexity, the French Method of preparing absinthe rivals the stylistic intricacies of the Japanese tea ritual.

This is no college-style premixed excrescence made by-the-vat and consumed by the gallon without any thought as to style or substance; these are professional alcoholics who glory in their rituals of decadence. The café is a place for discussion, debate, business, and oh yes, drinking; after all, what else could a sad little painter and his dancer friend do on a beautiful sunny day in a café overlooking *La Ville Lumière*.

The absinthe glass is specially designed with a large bulb-shaped reservoir at the bottom, a pinched-waist in the middle, and a more conventional upper portion that widens slightly towards the lip.

The redhead pours enough green colored absinthe to fill the reservoir of the glass. The slotted silver drip spoon is a complex design of cut out patterns for dripping, and a ridge along the edge so it sits securely in place on top of the odd shaped glass. The woman places a sugar cube on the spoon, and proceeds to pour ice water slowly over it, until the sugar disappears through the slots, and into the glass below. The absinthe mixture turns a milky green.

The result is called *louche*, and the process is designed to release the exotic aromas and flavors of the absinthe. This method of preparation is called the French Method, preferred in *La Belle Époque*, as opposed to the more modern Bohemian Method, where the sugar cube is pre-soaked in absinthe, set on fire, and dropped into the glass igniting the alcohol.

The flaming absinthe and sugar cube mixture is doused with ice water. The procedure produces a stronger drink. Sometimes the flaming absinthe is let to burn itself out; this cooking of the absinthe results in what is called *The Flaming Green Fairy*.

The Earthquake

How To Make An Earthquake
Tremblement de Terre
1. Add 3 parts of Absinthe to a Wine Goblet.
2. Add 3 parts of Cognac.

How To Make Death In The Afternoon
The great American novelist Ernest Hemingway was known to have invented several cocktails one of which was named after his book, *Death In The Afternoon*. The simple absinthe based cocktail is also known simply as the Hemingway.

The recipe was published in *So Red The Nose*, in 1935.
1. Pour 1 jigger of Absinthe into a Champagne Glass.
2. Add iced Champagne until it attains proper opalescent milkiness.
3. Drink 3 to 5 slowly (one assumes until either inspiration or coma ensues).

32
Absinthe

The history of absinthe is as exotic as *The French Method* of preparing it. Its reputation as a hallucinogen made it a popular subculture phenomenon in the bohemian artist communities, a reputation that got it unfairly banned for decades despite the fact that it is no more hallucinogenic than any other intoxicant.

Absinthe is a strong anise flavoured alcohol that comes from the leaves of the wormwood plant combined with green anise, sweet fennel, and assorted herbs. Absinthe, sometimes called, *la fée verte*, the green fairy owing to its traditional green color, can also be found in a colorless version, although the association with the color green is so strong I'm not sure why anyone would opt for the less flamboyant variety.

Although associated with France and the artistic residents of Montmartre it actually originated in Neuchatel, Switzerland in the seventeen hundreds. It later found its way to France where it gained popularity during the *La Bell Époque* amongst the bohemian painters, poets, and writers who were looking for a source of inspiration, or an escape from reality. Its mistaken reputation as a psychotropic hallucinogen added to its subculture popularity; but alas, any inspiration resulting from overindulgence was likely due to a combination of placebo induced expectations, and a potent ninety to one hundred and forty-eight proof alcohol content.

The consumption of absinthe grew until 1910 when its popularity overtook wine. The five o'clock after work tipple became known as *l'heure verte*, or the green hour. You can just imagine how the French wine industry reacted to that news. Absinthe was on a collision course with the wine industry and social conservatives. In 1905 a Swiss farmer named Jean Lanfry murdered his family after an alcoholic bender that included some small amounts of absinthe. The murders were blamed on the absinthe despite the fact Lanfry consumed large quantities of wine and brandy prior to a couple glasses of *la fée verte*.

Poorly conceived scientific studies on absinthe blamed the wild and sometimes dangerous behaviour of its adherents on the potentially mind-altering ingredient, thujone, a naturally occurring substance found in wormwood. More likely the bad behaviour of over indulgers was due to their alcoholism and not the trace amounts of thujone found in absinthe. The popular beverage became the social media bad-boy of its era, providing the temperance movement and its wine association allies with a cause célèbre, ultimately leading to a 1915 ban in the USA and most of Europe.

Although the bans on absinthe just about killed its popularity and consumer availability, there were pockets of resistance in various parts of Europe where it wasn't restricted and where it was still manufactured. Realizing Britain never banned absinthe, BBH Spirits began importing Hill's Absinthe from the Czech Republic in the 1990s. By 2011 even the French 1915 ban was finally lifted. Recent studies have proven that absinthe does not cause any psychotropic effects. Any previous incidents of uncontrollable behavior were more likely due to mere alcoholic over-indulgence, or consumption of cheap absinthe knockoffs that used poor quality, often toxic additional ingredients.

Absinthe

Traditional French Preparation
1. Fill the lower bowl of a special Absinthe Glass with Absinthe.
2. Place a specially designed slotted drip spoon over the Absinthe Glass containing the measure of Absinthe.
3. Place a sugar cube on top of a drip spoon.
4. Slowly pour, or drip ice water over the sugar cube until it dissolves (note: mix 2 oz of water into 1.5 oz of Absinthe).
5. The result is a flavourful, aromatic milky green liquid called *louche*.

Bohemian Method
1. Pre-soak a sugar cube in Absinthe.
2. Pour 1.5 oz of Absinthe into an Absinthe Glass.
3. Light the sugar cube on fire.
4. Drop the flaming sugar cube into the Absinthe Glass, igniting the Absinthe.
5. Put out the flaming Absinthe with 2 oz of cold water, or just let the fire burn its self out. This method creates a stronger drink than the French Method. If the Absinthe is allowed to extinguish by itself without the water, the variation is called "Cooking the Absinthe" or "The Flaming Green Fairy."

The Bohemian method is a dangerous fire hazard due to the high alcohol content in the Absinthe.

The Experience

The fascinating thing about cocktails is how much creativity goes into their creation; like a work of art, color, texture, and presentation are used to enhance the taste, smell, and experience. And like works of art that hang in a gallery; where you experience these exotic pleasures has as much to do with the experience as any of the other ingredients.

There will always be those who drink to get drunk as if it was a sport; those that drink to drown their sorrows; and those that drink in the hope of some flash of insight. But somewhere there are those who see cocktails as an expression of art, in the same way as great chefs see their creations as an expression of culinary virtuosity. Too much... perhaps, but the fact is those that take the time to name their creations with some inventive forethought have added to the pleasures of consumption beyond the adolescent goal of getting hammered. The dangers of alcohol are well known, and over-indulgence has caused many hardships, and fostered innumerable self-destructive behaviours.

A cocktail should be more than just a way to quench one's thirst; it should be an experience with a history and a story to tell; and the name given to each variation is where it all begins. But there is one more element that adds to the experience and pleasure, and that is the environment. Bar and restaurant owners go to great expense to deliver an atmosphere that adds to the experience. There are unique bars and restaurants all over the world, some comfortable, some rustic, some entertaining, some artful, some exotic, and some just plain bizarre.

Cabaret de L'Enfer

33
Cabaret de L'Enfer
Cabaret of Hell

The Boulevard de Clichy, 1890, the red-light district of Montmartre, Paris. The area is home to the famous Moulin Rouge as well as the many artists and bohemians who find the cheap rents and decadent pleasures a readily available source of inspiration, comradeship, and over-indulgence. The street is home to one of the first themed restaurants, the *Cabaret de L'Enfer*, the Cabaret of Hell. The place is, as much a carnival sideshow as it is a bar, but then again, is it any more contrived than the colorful Carousel Bar in New Orleans?

A Mephistopheles-inspired doorman stands guard in front of a grotesque carved open-mouthed demon that encircles the entrance. Above the monster and surrounding the iron barred windows are assorted naked cavorting evil spirits carved into a moulded exterior of dripping decay. The inside is no less bizarre. Patrons order their cognac-spiked coffees from devil-costumed waiters who shout out instructions to the kitchen demanding: "seething bumpers of molten sins, with a dash of brimstone intensifier."

Other guests sit sipping their molten sins while hideous carved devil-like creatures hang precariously just above their heads. If the scene isn't already creepy enough, a demon clad ensemble of male and female musicians play selections from *Faust*. It may all seem a bit tame and silly by today's standards but back in the 1890s this was the height of existential depravity. As unique and thoroughly bizarre as the *Cabaret de L'Enfer* was, it was not the only weird mind-bending drinking establishment in the area.

Cabaret du Néant

34
Cabaret du Néant
Cabaret of Nothingness

William Chambers Morrows in his book, *Bohemian Paris of Today*, appears to have the best account of the goings on within the *Cabaret du Néant*, the Cabaret of Nothingness, or if you prefer, the Cabaret of Death. The black front door is illuminated only by two iron lanterns giving off an eerie green glow that reflects on the faces of anyone who dares enter. The way in is draped in black shrouds or cerements with white trim and patrolled by a black-caped undertaker inspired guardian in a glazed top hat.

As guests make their way through the black shrouded entrance, they notice a bizarre chandelier, seemingly constructed from the bones of perhaps an unsatisfied customer. Guests follow a monk-like character along a darkened hallway until they come to a room filled with tables shaped like coffins.

The coffins rest on moveable frames called biers used for displaying the recently deceased. Symbols of death decorate the walls as if you already didn't get the message. Mysterious voices drone on in the background with some ominous chant. Waiters dressed in *croque-mort* funeral attire complete with black claw-hammer coats welcome guests with: *"Bon soir Macchabees!"* a bizarre greeting generally reserved for sailors who find cadavers floating in the water.

Okay this stuff is weird, but it gets even better or worse depending on your point of view. After enjoying a drink of choice, guests are told to look closely at the paintings on the wall; the figures in the paintings gradually turn into skeletons.

The monk accompanied by a funeral dirge leads the guests to another room where a volunteer is instructed to step on stage. The poor fellow is wrapped in a shroud and placed in an upright coffin for viewing. By some nineteenth century optical trickery the volunteer is turned into a skeleton before the eyes of his terrified friends. Gradually the volunteer returns to normal and patrons are ushered into the last chamber where seemingly live skeletons walk around another poor soul who dared volunteer.

H. R. Giger

35
The Giger Bar

Cabaret L'Enfer and Cabaret du Néant seem both silly and out-of-date by today's standards, but today, themed experience-oriented bars can be found everywhere. Continuing the theme of creepy, the two Giger Bars, designed by Swiss artist H. R. Giger seem to meet the criteria of strange and different. Giger, of course, is the artist best known for his work in designing the monsters in the *Alien* movie franchise.

Entering the Giger bar one gets the impression that you've entered the belly of the monster, with the carved arched ceiling reminiscent of the skeletal infrastructure of the beast. The high-backed throne-like chairs surround and consume the guest with what appears to be an alien rib cage. The floors appear etched in some bizarre biomechanical diagrammatic blueprint of monster construction. A large framed silver wall-hanging sculpture appears to be some kind of alien weapon that fires goggled mini monster bullets, with three in the clip and one in the chamber. Various other sculptures of sexy female mechanical *cyborgian* creatures appear around every corner. The place is as much a Giger museum as it is a bar; the scene is assuredly fantastical.

Perhaps these examples of themed drinking establishments are more about the experience of the environment, than they are an epicurean interest in what they serve, but then again, if consumption of vast quantities of alcohol was your only interest, why not just curl up in a corner with a bottle of Thunderbird?

General Pascal Olivier Count de Negroni

36
The Negroni

It shouldn't surprise you by now to know that the origin of the Negroni is disputed like many other famous cocktails. It seems once a drink finds a substantial following, pretenders line up to take credit for its creation. In the case of the Negroni, there are two versions of how this cocktail came into being.

The first version attributes the creation to Count Camilio Negroni in Florence in 1919. It seems Negroni was in the mood for something stiff to drink so he asked the Caffe Casoni bartender, Fosco Scarselli, to add gin to his Americano rather than the usual soda water. Scarselli added an orange garnish in order to distinguish it from the Americano's typical lemon garnish. The drink became so successful that the Negroni family started the Negroni Distillerie in order to produce a ready-made version of his creation. The Negroni grew in popularity and became a favorite among influential media savvy Americans like actor, director, and bon vivant extraordinaire, Orson Welles, who discovered the drink while in Rome around 1947.

The second pretender to the Negroni creation is a French speaking Corsican, General Pascal Olivier Count de Negroni, Count de Negroni takes credit for creating the drink at either the St. Augustine Officers' Club just prior to WWI or at the Lunéville Officers Club in 1870.

The descendents of Pascal Negroni claim Camilio didn't even exist, however records seem to show that Camilio travelled to New York in 1892 at age twenty-nine where he appears to be listed in a local directory as a fencing instructor. Eventually he returned to Italy were he claims to have invented the drink. On the other hand Pascal's family puts forth an accredited letter, hand-written in 1857 where Pascal writes "Incidentally, did you know that the vermouth-based cocktail that I invented in Saint Louis is a great hit at the Lunéville officers club?"

One final piece of useless trivia, the forerunner of the Negroni, the Americano, was the first drink ordered by James Bond in Ian Flemings' novel *Casino Royale*, as well as in the short story, *From a View to a Kill*. Even though Bond ordered the Americano he insisted on the bartender using Perrier and not just any cheap soda water, as expensive soda water, according to Bond, was the best way to improve a poor drink, something to remember when you want to signal to your friends that you truly are a cocktail snob.

The mixture that became known as the Americano was first created at the Caffe Camparino in the 1860s and originally called the Milano-Torino because Campari came from Milan and Sweet Vermouth from Turin. During prohibition the drink became a favorite of many travelling Americans and thus became known as the Americano. On the other hand, the name may have been derived from the Italian word, *amaro*, meaning bitter, describing the taste of the Campari.

The Negroni

How To Make A Negroni
1. Add 1 oz of Gin to a shaker containing ice.
2. Add 1 oz of Campari.
3. Add 1 oz of Sweet Vermouth
4. Add a Grapefruit or Orange Peel.
5. Stir & strain into an Old Fashion Glass over ice.
6. Garnish with an Orange Peel.

How To Make An Americano
1. Add 1.5 oz of Campari to a Mixing Glass.
2. Add 1.5 oz of Sweet Vermouth.
3. Pour into an Old Fashion Glass over ice.
4. Add a splash of Soda Water.
5. Garnish with a half of an Orange Slice.

37
The Singapore Sling

Ngiam Tong Boon, a Hainanese bartender, created the Singapore Sling at the famous Long Bar in the Raffles Hotel, Singapore. It was originally called a Gin Sling; a Sling referred to an American drink of spirit and water, sweetened and flavoured.

How To Make The Singapore Sling
1. Add 1.5 oz of Dry Gin to a shaker with ice.
2. Add .25 oz of Benedictine.
3. Add .5 oz of Cherry Heering.
4. Add .25 oz of Cointreau Liqueur
5. Add 4 oz of Pineapple Juice.
6. Add .5 oz of Lime Juice.
7. Add .334 oz of Grenadine.
8. Add 1 dash of bitters.
9. Shake & strain into Collins Glass with crushed ice.
10. Fill with Soda if desired.
11. Garnish with a slice of Pineapple or Cherry

Other cocktails named after famous places include: the Manhattan, the Blue Hawaiian, the Alabama Slammer, the Sweating Columbian, the Harlem Mugger, the White Russian, the Moscow Mule, the London Buck, Long Island Ice Tea, the Berlin Martini, the Parisian, the Tennessee Cowboy, the Amsterdam Cocktail, the Chicago Fizz, and the Flaming Mexican Flag.

Ada Coleman

Rubert D'Oyly Carte

Cocktails and Sex

You can find cocktails named after just about everything including sex; some are clever, some are funny, and some are just plain raunchy. I suppose it's inevitable that left to their devices, creative bartenders would eventually get around to putting a little sex into the handbook of mixology.

Here's a list of down and dirty drink names that I dare you to order in mixed company, and yes they're all actual cocktails with published recipes: the Screaming Orgasm, Sex On The Beach, Bend Over Shirley, Adios Motherfucker, Blue Balls, Angel's Tit, Red-Headed Slut, Mountain Dew Me, Sex With An Alligator, Between the Sheets, *Ménage a Trois*, Afternoon Delight, Buttery Nipple, Climax, and Liquid Viagra.

I kid you not, they all exist, and there are more with even sleazier names. The history behind many of these names was never recorded, probably for good reason, however there are a couple that do have interesting back-stories of historical interest.

38
The Hanky Panky

The Hanky Panky is one of the tamer names given to this category of cocktails, and unlike some sex-named cocktails that were named just for fun, or perhaps, for sheer shock-value, this one actually has an interesting history, at least one we can talk about.

Today female bartenders are commonplace but in the late nineteenth and early twentieth centuries bartending was not considered a suitable occupation for a nice young lady. A 1895 US census listed 55,660 male bartenders and only 147 females. Whenever there's a prohibition of some kind there's always a few brave souls willing to challenge it; and we can find one of these barrier breakers in London's Savoy Hotel.

Ada Coleman wasn't the first female bartender at the Savoy that distinction goes to Ruth Burgess. I imagine she must have been well liked and good at her job since the hotel's owner Rupert D'Oyly Carte, whose family produced the Gilbert and Sullivan operas, went out and hired a second female bartender, Ada Coleman. The two women were quickly dubbed Kitty and Coley by the London press.

Ada or Coley as she was known was very popular and had a creative knack for developing new cocktails. One of Coley's regulars was famous actor Sir Charles Henry Hawtry who was ultimately responsible for inspiring Coleman's signature creation. Ada Coleman described the creation and naming of her signature mix of gin, Italian vermouth and Fernet Branca in a 1925 article published in *The People* newspaper:

"The late Charles Hawtrey... was one of the best judges of cocktails that I knew. Some years ago, when he was overworking, he used to come into the bar and say, 'Coley, I am tired. Give me something with a bit of punch in it.' It was for him that I spent hours experimenting until I had invented a new cocktail. The next time he came in, I told him I had

a new drink for him. He sipped it, and, draining the glass, he said, 'By Jove! That is the real hanky-panky!' And Hanky-Panky it has been called ever since."

In 1919 the United States passed the 18th Amendment to the Constitution resulting in a series of unintended consequences, including the creation of the financial driving force behind the rise of organized crime. Poor Ada was just collateral damage. In order to appease their prudish American clientele who felt female bartenders were unseemly, D'Oyly Carte dismissed Kitty and transferred Coley to the flower shop, supposedly a much more appropriate occupation for a woman of the early nineteen hundreds.

Ada's place, as head bartender at the Savoy's American Bar, was taken by Harry Craddock who went on to become one of the most famous bartenders of the 20s and 30s. Craddock invented several classic cocktails including the Corpse Reviver #2 and the White Lady. His book, *The Savoy Cocktail Book* is still in print, and is regarded as an essential component of any serious mixologist's library. Craddock also co-founded the United Kingdom Bartenders' Guild.

If not for the Hanky Panky cocktail, Ada Coleman's place in cocktail history, not to mention her groundbreaking challenge to a male dominated occupation, would be lost to time. Unfortunately despite all of Harry Craddock's achievements he didn't fair any better. After a long and productive career he died in 1963 and is buried in a pauper's grave, sharing it with two other men.

The Hanky Panky

How To Make Ada's Hanky Panky
1. Add 1.5 oz of Cognac to a shaker with ice.
2. Add 1.5 oz of Sweet Vermouth.
3. Add 2 dashes of Fernet Branca.
4. Stir, strain, and pour into Coupe Glass.
5. Garnish with an Orange Peel.

Note: The Harry Craddock version in The Savoy Cocktail Book uses Dry Gin rather than Cognac.

The Corpse Reviver

Harry Craddock's Corpse Reviver #2
The Corpse Reviver #2 is one of a series of hangover cures with the Corpse Reviver name; this is Harry Craddock's version.

How To Make A Corpse Reviver #2
1. Add 1 oz of Gin to an ice filled cocktail shaker.
2. Add 1 oz of Lillet Blanc.
3. Add 1 oz of fresh squeezed Lime Juice
4. Add 1 oz of Cointreau.
5. Add 1 drop of Absinthe.
6. Shake and strain into a chilled Martini Glass.
7. Garnish with a Cherry.

Harry Craddock

Harry MacElhone

39
The White Lady and The Duelling Harrys

The White Lady cocktail is another drink with a disputed heritage. Harry MacElhone, another famous barkeep, claims to be the first to come up with the original recipe using Crème de Menthe in 1919 at London's Ciro's Club. He later claims to have refined his recipe by substituting Gin for the Crème de Menthe while working at his Harry's New York Bar in Paris.

The history of Harry's New York Bar in Paris is also interesting on its own. The bar still exists and you can visit it at 5, Rue Daunou in Paris. The place was originally owned by an American jockey named Tod Sloan. He bought a Paris bistro in 1911 and converted it into what he called the New York Bar. Sloan had a partner who owned a bar in New York. Together they had the New York bar dismantled and sent to Paris where it was reassembled. American expatriates in the creative communities were flocking to Paris at that time and Sloan thought he could cash in by giving his fellow Yanks a taste of home. He hired Harry MacElhone to run the bar.

Sloan liked to live high-on-the-hog and eventually ran into financial trouble. In 1923 MacElhone took over the place and renamed it Harry's New York Bar. The place became a hotspot for famous actors, personalities, and jetsetters. Harry MacElhone created numerous cocktails including the already discussed Monkey's Gland. Among the famous personalities that found their way to Harry's was George Gershwin, who supposedly wrote his seminal piece *An American in Paris* at the Ivories Piano Bar in Harry's.

Harry Craddock's claim to the White Lady comes in his seminal cocktail primer *The Savoy Cocktail Book*, first published in 1930. Harry MacElhone claims he invented the initial recipe in 1919 and refined it in 1929.

How To Make Harry MacElhone's White Lady
1. Add 1.5 oz of London Dry Gin to a shaker with ice.
2. Add .75 oz of Triple Sec Liqueur (Orange Liqueur).
3. Add .75 oz of fresh squeezed Lemon Juice.
4. Add .334 oz Sugar Syrup (2 parts sugar to 1 water).
5. Add 1 Fresh Egg White (not part of MacElhone's original recipe found in his *Harry's ABC of Mixing Cocktails* book.)
6. Shake with ice.
7. Strain into second shaker removing the ice.
8. Shake again without ice.
9. Strain into a chilled Martini Glass.
10. Garnish with a Lemon twist.

How To Make Harry Craddock's White Lady
1. Add 2 oz of London Dry Gin to a shaker with no ice.
2. Add .5 oz of Cointreau (Orange Liqueur).
3. Add .5 oz of fresh squeezed Lemon Juice.
4. Add 1 Fresh Egg White (not part of Craddock's original recipe found in his 1930 *The Savoy Cocktail Book*).
5. Shake without ice.
6. Add ice and shake again.
7. Fine-strain into a chilled Martini Glass.

40
Sex On The Beach

The White Lady got us a little sidetracked; I believe we were discussing sex, so how about a little sex on the beach, just don't forget to bring your sunscreen? Like several other cocktails Sex On The Beach was created as a result of some marketing guy's efforts to sell more peach schnapps. The time was spring 1987, and college students, as they do every year, were chomping, or if you prefer champing at the bit to head on down to Florida for Spring Break: a legendary time of sun, fun, and sex.

In order to move more schnapps the distributor decided to have a contest awarding the bar that sold the most peach schnapps a thousand dollars, and the bartender with the highest sales a hundred bucks. According to the Sex On The Beach Drinks Company, a young bartender at the Confetti Bar came up with a peach schnapps, vodka, orange juice, and grenadine combo that metaphorically and literally knocked the socks off the young undergrads, as well as other garments one presumes. When the young bartender was asked what he called his new concoction, he thought for a second, and realizing that college students on Spring Break come to Florida for two reasons, the beach and sex, he dubbed his creation Sex On The Beach.

How To Make Sex On The Beach
1. Fill a Highball glass with ice.
2. Add 1.334 oz of Vodka.
2. Add 1.334 oz of Cranberry Juice.
3. Add .667 oz of Peach Schnapps.
4. Add 1.334 oz of Orange Juice
5. Garnish with Orange Slice and Maraschino Cherry.

Robert Rosebud Butt

41
Long Island Iced Tea

At first glance a cocktail named the Long Island Iced Tea seems kind of strange, but then it may make more sense after we investigate its origins, and yes it appears to have multiple beginnings. It seems most likely the drink we call the Long Island Iced Tea was actually invented twice. Sounds weird, but when you think about the muddled history of cocktails, it is the most likely case.

Robert Rosebud Butt, bartender at the Oak Beach Inn on Long Island, NY takes credit for its invention as an entrant to a 1972 contest that called for new cocktails that included Triple Sec. Of course another barkeep at the Oak Beach Inn, Chris Bendicksen, also claims to be the inventor. The story may actually be true but if it is, how do you explain the fact that a recipe for Long Island Ice Tea can be found in *Betty Crocker's New Picture Cook Book* published in 1961.

Enter Old Man Bishop a resident of Long Island, Kingsport, Tennessee, who claims to have invented the drink in the Prohibition era of the 1920s. Old Man Bishop passed the recipe of whiskey, maple syrup, plus five additional liqueurs onto his son Ransom Bishop who claims to have perfected the combination of ingredients.

Considering the Betty Crocker recipe published in 1961, the Long Island Tennessee location, and the fact the cocktail is designed to look like Prohibition-safe tea, all make for a strong case in believing Ransom Bishop's claim. With revenuers around every corner during the 1920s, ordering a Long Island Iced Tea, a drink that actually looks like you're sipping tea, makes a lot of sense. The most likely answer to the controversy is that both stories are true.

How To Make Rosebud's Long Island Iced Tea

1. Add 2 cups of ice cubes to a Highball Glass
2. Add 1.5 oz of Vodka.
3. Add 1.5 oz of Gin.
4. Add 1.5 oz of White Rum.
5. Add 1.5 oz of White Tequila.
6. Add .75 oz of Triple Sec.
7. Add .75 oz of Sour Mix (Substitute Lemon Juice).
8. Add 1 Splash of Cola Soda.
9. Garnish with a Lemon Wedge.

How To Make Ransom Bishop's Long Island Iced Tea

1. Squeeze .5 a fresh Lemon into a shaker with ice.
2. Squeeze .5 a fresh Lime into a shaker.
3. Add .5 oz of Rum.
4. Add 1 oz of Vodka.
5. Add 1 oz of Whiskey.
6. Add .5 oz of Gin.
7. Add .5 oz of Tequila.
8. Add .5 oz of Maple Syrup.
9. Mix Thoroughly.
10. Add 4 to 5 oz of Cola Soda.

42
Irish Coffee

You can generally categorize people into two groups, tea drinkers and coffee drinkers, not that a coffee drinker will never have a tea, or vice versa, but chances are everyone has a definite preference. Since we've already discussed tea's alcohol namesake, it is only right that we do the same for coffee. Although Long Island Iced Tea contains no tea, Irish Coffee does contain coffee. It is interesting to note that the Irish are great tea and whiskey drinkers, but coffee, not so much.

The restaurant in the Monteagle Arms Hotel located in the terminal building at Foynes Flying Boat Airport 1943, houses the newly opened restaurant run by Brendan O'Regan. It is considered one of the best restaurants in Ireland despite the fact the village of Foynes has a population of less than five hundred people. But during the war, strategic location was far more important than population size, and with strategic importance comes important people.

Chef Joe Sheridan of Castlederg, County knew things had to be just right for the military and celebrity clientele that used the airport as a jumping off point for travelling to Europe and North America. Those that passed through Foynes included Hollywood actors like Humphrey Bogart and Edward G. Robinson, politicians like Anthony Eden and Eleanor Roosevelt, and royalty like Queen Wilhelmina of Holland and King George of Greece.

The Night The Irish Reinvented Coffee

It's a miserable night and the foul weather matches the moods of the passengers that had taken off for Botwood, Nfld several hours earlier. The weather is so bad the Captain decides to return to Foynes even though they were several hours out. He informs the tower at Foynes by Morse Code that he is returning to wait for the weather to clear. The control tower informs the staff at the hotel. O'Regan and Sheridan scramble to prepare food and drinks for the cold frustrated passengers who would certainly not be in the best of moods.

O'Regan tells Sheridan to put something together that would warm up the passengers bodies and spirits. Sheridan prepares hot coffee and decides that a good measure of Irish Whiskey added to the coffee might just do the trick. Once the passengers arrive they settle down for some good food and Sheridan's hot coffee and whiskey creation. The new beverage is a hit with the travellers and one fellow inquires whether the coffee being served is Brazilian Coffee, to which Sheridan replies, "No... that was Irish Coffee!" The response to the makeshift warmer-upper is so good Sheridan decides to put his creation in a stemmed glass and serve it as a new offering in the restaurant.

The Foynes Flying Boat Airport was ultimately replaced by the more modern Shannon Airport when land based aircraft with longer ranges replaced the seaplanes that dominated the 1930s and early 1940s. You can replace an airport but replacing a classic like Irish Coffee is much harder. Dignitaries that fly out of Shannon are still served Sheridan's Irish Coffee. As a matter of interest, there is a difference between *whiskey* and *whisky*. The term *whisky* refers solely to Scotch whisky, while the term *whiskey* refers to either Irish or American whiskey,

Irish Coffee

How To Make The Original Irish Coffee
1. Warm a stemmed Whiskey Goblet.
2. Add 2 oz of Irish Whiskey.
3. Add 2 teaspoons of brown sugar, stir to dissolve.
4. Fill with freshly brewed black coffee.
5. For a modern touch, not used in the original, top off with whipped. Let the whipped cream sit on top and sip the coffee through the whipped cream. Alternatively, if whipped cream is not for you, you can pour fresh pouring cream over the back of a spoon so it floats on top of the coffee and whiskey mixture.

Irish Variations With Coffee

Irish Cream Café
1, Pour .5 oz Bushmills Irish Cream into a tall glass.
2. Add .5 oz of Coffee Liqueur.
3. Add .5 oz of Hazelnut Liqueur.
4. Add 6 oz of Coffee.
5. Add Whipped Cream and a Cinnamon Stick.

Drowned Irish Coffee

1. Brew .5 a cup of Hot Espresso.
2. Dissolve 1 tsp of sugar into the Espresso.
3. Pour into a small plastic cup & freeze till solid.
4. Scrape the frozen mixture to make icy crystals.
5. Spoon the crystals into a glass.
6. Add 2 oz of Baileys Irish Cream.
7. Add more crystals on top.
8. Garnish with a Lemon Twirl & serve with a spoon.

Irish Tiramisu For 2

This bit of extravagance is more of a dessert than it is a cocktail, but if you're trying to impress a dinner guest who has more of a sweet tooth than a taste for alcohol, then this baby is for you.

1. Add .25 of a cup Espresso to a blender.
2. Add 4 oz of Baileys Irish Cream.
3. Add .334 cup of Mascarpone Cheese
4. Add 2 scoops of Vanilla, Chocolate or Coffee Ice Cream.
5. Add 2 to 4 ice cubes and blend till smooth.
6. Decorate the sides of two oversized Martini Glasses with chocolate syrup.
7. Rim glasses with chocolate syrup by dipping the glass in a plate with chocolate syrup (if desired).
8. Pour the blended mixture into the Martini Glasses.
9. Serve with ladyfingers sliced in half and reassembled with chocolate-hazelnut spread in-between.
10. If you want to be really decadent add whip cream to the top.

43
Screech
A Newfoundland Elixir from Jamaica

When it comes to alcohol Canada may be best known for Canadian whiskey or rye with its distinct lighter, smoother flavor as compared to other whiskies that don't add rye to their mashes. The history of Canadian whiskey is well documented with its reputation enhanced by its Prohibition era export/smuggling into the USA.

Even though Prohibition existed in Canada, its length was short, and its enforcement was at best sporadic. Add to that, the fact that alcohol could be legally produced and exported, but not sold domestically in Canada, helped cement the country's reputation and place in alcohol history. But Canadian rye whiskey is not the only alcohol beverage with an interesting Canadian past.

Before any government interference, Newfoundland fisherman shipped salt fish to the West Indies in return for rum. The no-name imported Jamaican rum became the drink of choice among the hard working Newfoundland fisherman who enjoyed the rum in large quantities at an extremely potent strength.

During WWII thirsty American servicemen were stationed in Newfoundland. According to Screech legend one brave GI tried the local unbranded rum by downing his drink in one gulp, not realizing the potency of the no-name local favorite. The poor soldier yelled out in distress causing his colleagues to come rushing to his aid. "What the cripes was that ungodly screech?" To which one local fisherman replied "The screech? Tis the rum, me son." And so a new brand of rum was born, Screech Rum.

The Metropolitan Screech
1. Add 2 oz of Screech Rum to a shaker with ice.
2. Add 2 oz of Cranberry Juice.
3. Add .5 oz of Orange Liqueur.
4. Add Juice from 1 Lime.
5. Shake and strain into a Martini Glass
6. Add a splash of Club Soda.
7. Garnish with a Lime Wedge.

The Traditional Metropolitan
1. Add 2 oz of Brandy to shaker with crushed ice.
2. Add .5 oz of Sweet Vermouth.
3. Add 1 dash of bitters.
4. Add 1 tsp of superfine sugar.
5. Shake and strain into Martini Glass.

The Muffled
1. Place ice cubes in a glass.
2. Layer 1 oz of Screech Rum.
3. Layer .25 oz of Triple Sec or Grand Marnier.
4. Layer 2 oz of Cream on top.

The Storm
1. Add 2 oz of Screech to a Highball Glass with ice.
2. Fill with of Ginger Beer.
3. Squeeze in a slice of Lime.
4. To make a 'Perfect Storm' add 2 dashes of Angostura Bitters.

William (The Real) McCoy, Prohibition Smuggler

44
Cocktails That Could Burn Your House Down

There is a whole series of cocktails that people light on fire for some reason, one assumes to enhance the flavour, to strengthen the potency, to create a flashy presentation, or maybe just to collect the insurance money. There must be a lot of pyromaniacs out there because there are dozens of cocktails that somebody has decided to set on fire. We've already talked about the *Flaming Green Fairy* but there are more, a lot more, but before we go any further, be forewarned, lighting alcohol on fire is dangerous, and if you're drunk, it's downright stupid.

If all you want to do is impress your girlfriend with an ostentatious display of showy self-indulgence, buy her a diamond, it's safer. If you want to try one of these burnt offerings, order it in a bar or restaurant from a bartender that knows what he or she is doing and who has experience.

According to Nate Steere, in his article *How (And Why) To Set Drinks On Fire* published on askmen.com, there is something called the 80 proof rule: any alcohol that's 80 proof or over will light. This includes tequila, rum, whiskey, and vodka. According to Steere some liquors under 80 proof can also be set on fire depending on other factors like sugar content. Here's a few hot numbers you can order to impress your hot date, just make sure she carries a fire extinguisher with her in her purse: the Flaming Giraffe, the Flaming Gorilla, the Flaming Martini, the

B-52, the Flaming Volcano, the Hanukkah Miracle, and my personal favourite based solely on the marshmallow garnish, the Flaming S'more Martini.

The Flaming Giraffe

(Order from a professional bartender – Dangerous!)
1. Add 2 oz of Kahlua liqueur to a Double Shot Glass.
2. Add 1 oz of Butterscotch Schnapps.
3. Float 1 oz of Bacardi 151 Proof Rum on top.
4. Set on fire but blow out and let cool before drinking - really, some people actually need this instruction.

Here are a few fun cocktails with or without the pyrotechnics that are not for the serious cocktail aficionado, but can be an entertaining drink to order.

The Flaming S'more Martini

(Order from a professional bartender – Dangerous!)
1. Rim a Martini glass with chocolate syrup.
2. Coat the rim with Graham Cracker Crumbs.
3. Add 1 oz of Crème de Cacao to an ice filled shaker.
4. Add 1 oz of Marshmallow Vodka to the shaker.
5. Add 1 oz of Irish Cream.
6. Add 1 oz of Heavy Cream.
7. Shake and strain into a Martini glass.
8. Float either Bacardi 151 or Everclear on top.
9. Pierce a marshmallow with a cocktail stick so the marshmallow rests in the Bacardi 151 and set on fire to roast the marshmallow. You can also toast the marshmallow beforehand without the Bacardi but then you kind of miss the whole point of the exercise.

Not every splashy drink presentation needs to involve setting things on fire. Here are a couple of options that may be high in calories but don't involve any flame retardant extras.

The Cotton Candy Martini

This one doesn't involve any flames, but it makes for a goofy potent gimmick drink for your friends who have a sweet tooth.
1. Fill a shaker halfway with ice.
2. Add 2 oz of Cotton Candy Vodka.
3. Add 1 oz of Pineapple Juice.
4. Add 1 oz of Cranberry Juice.
5. Add a splash of Grenadine.
6. Fill a Martini glass with Cotton Candy.
7. Shake & strain into Martini Glass over the Cotton Candy. The Cotton Candy will instantly dissolve. Finally, garnish with a touch of Cotton Candy for flare.

The Angel's Kiss

The Angel's Kiss is a simple two-ingredient drink if prepared properly will pucker up like your sweetheart after she tastes your romantic display of affection.
1. Add 2 oz of Dark Crème de Cacao to a Martini glass.
2. Carefully float Cream over the top of a spoon so it rests on top of the Crème de Cacao, if done right the cream will pucker.

Forgotten Gems

Everybody, well not everybody, but people who like to imbibe tend to have a favourite drink, but if you're adventurous, you can reach back into the history books, blow off the dust, and order a concoction from the good old days. If you really want to check out some long-forgotten cocktails checkout Ted Haigh's book, *Vintage Spirits and Forgotten Cocktails*. Many of these recipes and more can be found on adrinkontherocks.com/vintage-cocktails.

45
The Leatherneck

The term Leatherneck refers to US Marines. The nickname goes back to the Revolutionary War when Marines wore uniforms with high leather collars that were supposed to protect them from sword wounds. I'm not sure a piece of leather would do the trick but perhaps it provided some sense of comfort to the soldiers. According to Ted Haigh, the Leatherneck cocktail was invented by a former Marine and *New York World-Telegram* columnist Frank Farrell.

How To Make A Leatherneck
1. Add 2 oz of Blended Whiskey to a shaker with ice.
2. Add .75 oz of Blue Curacao.
3. Add .5 oz of Lime Juice.
4. Shake and strain into a Cocktail Glass.
5. Garnish with a Lime Wheel.

46
The Lion's Tail

Here's another discovery you can find in Haigh's *Vintage Spirits and Forgotten Cocktails*. It was originally seen in the 1937 edition of the *Café Royal Cocktail Book*. The name seems to have come from some unknown American expatriate living in England. The lion has long been a symbol associated with Britain. The expression, *twist the lion's tail*, seemed to be a favourite of Americans living in Great Britain in the 1930s. The expression means to tax the patience or provoke a person, group, or government, especially that of Great Britain.

How To Make A Lion's Tail
1. Add 2 oz of Bourbon to a shaker with ice.
2. Add .5 oz of Lime Juice.
3. Add .5 oz of Allspice Liqueur.
4. Add 1 teaspoon of Simple Syrup.
5. Add 2 dashes of Angostura Bitters.
6. Shake and strain into a Cocktail Glass.
7. Optionally garnish with a Lime Wheel.

47
The Japalac Cocktail

The recipe for this strangely named cocktail from 1931, first appeared in Albert Stevens Crockett's, *Old Waldorf Bar Days*. According to Haig, Japalac was a quick drying varnish sold by the Glidden Company. Why this particular combination of drinkable ingredients was named after a varnish is unknown but if you're looking for a cocktail that will no doubt stump your hipster bartender, this might be a good choice.

How To Make A Japalac
1. Add .75 oz of Dry Vermouth to a shaker with ice.
2. Add .75 oz of Rye Whiskey.
3. Add 1 teaspoon of Raspberry Syrup.
4. Squeeze .25 of an Orange into mixture
5. Add 2 dashes of Angostura Bitters.
6. Shake and strain into a small glass.
7. Garnish with an Orange Twist.

48
The Twelve-Mile Limit Cocktail

During Prohibition alcohol was illegal on American soil as well as up to three miles out to sea. If you were further out than three miles, you could legally indulge or transport alcohol. The original three-mile limit was a rather low bar for smugglers and creative drinkers to overcome. To celebrate their creative legal trickery the Three Mile Limit Cocktail was invented, a mixture of rum cognac, grenadine, and lemon juice. Realizing the three-mile prohibition wasn't working the government increased it to twelve miles, and of course that meant a new Twelve-Mile Limit cocktail had to be created.

How To Make A Twelve-Mile Limit

1. Add 1 oz of White Rum to a shaker with ice.
2. Add .5 oz of Rye Whiskey.
3. Add .5 oz of Brandy.
4. Add .5 oz of Grenadine.
5. Add .5 oz of freshly squeezed Lemon Juice.
6. Shake and strain into a Cocktail Glass
7. Garnish with a Lemon Twist.

49
The Alamagoozlum Cocktail

I could not end this book without adding one more delightful name to the list of crazy drinkable histories. The Alamagoozlum was created by J. P. Morgan, the renowned banker and corporate titan. Morgan was instrumental in putting together the complex mergers that formed General Electric and the US Steel Corporation.

Like his business mergers his liquid creation is a complicated collection of ingredients forming a complex merging of tastes. The Alamagoozlum recipe was published in 1939 by Charles H Baker in *The Gentlemen's Companion or Around the World with Jigger, Beaker and Flask.*

According to worldwidewords.org Alamagoozlum may be the combination of the French à *la* and *goozlum*, which is either cowboy slang for guts as in "I hate your *goozlum*," or more likely

J. P. Morgan

meaning thick sauces, gravy, or syrups. It might also be derived from the word *magoozlum*, meaning hooey or nonsense. And finally there is the theory that the name came from the cartoon character *Mr. Magoo*, with *magoo* referring to movie jargon for the filling of custard pies used in slapstick comedies.

How To Make An Alamagoozlum
1. Add 2 oz of Genever Gin to a shaker with ice.
2. Add 2 oz of Water.
3. Add 1.5 oz of Jamaican Rum.
4. Add 1.5 oz of Chartreuse.
5. Add 1.5 oz of Gomme Syrup (Simple Syrup).
6. Add .5 oz of Orange Curacao.
7. Add .5 oz of Angostura Bitters.
8. Add .5 of an Egg White.
9. Shake and strain into a chilled Cocktail Glass.

The Cocktail Name Game

Naming cocktails is an art. There are so many cocktail variations that it's hard for a poor bartender to keep up; but if you look, you can find creative mixologists who can't help but search for the Holy Grail of taste combinations. And what would a great cocktail be if it didn't have a great name to go along with it.

There are drinks named after just about everything: people, like The Negroni, occupations, like The Mariner's Ghost, animals, like The Nut Bunny, places, like The Singapore Sling, and sex, like The Hanky Panky. There are drinks named after exotic animals like The Tiger Paw and The Flaming Giraffe; there are drinks named after mythical animals like The Trojan Horse and The Red Dragon's Breath; and there are drinks named after man's best friend like The Salty Dog and The Bulldog Smash.

How most of these cocktails got their names is lost to history. My guess is they just plain sounded cool, or the inventor had some affinity for the creature, place, or person in question. A number of drinks like The Brass Monkey found their origin in marketing campaigns. According to cocktail writer and historian David Wondrich, The Pink Squirrel was a 1950s marketing campaign for a cocktail made from a pink almond liqueur and crème de cacao, The campaign was based on a sexy young woman walking into bars with a pink-coloured squirrel on a leash.

Come up with a name, and there is probably already a drink named after it. If you're looking for a wide variety of options from which to choose an appropriately named favorite, you can check out tuxedono2.com. The website lists many colourful recipes.

Random Cocktail Recipes With Interesting Names

There are a lot more cocktails you can discover on the Internet, however my interest is in the history and how they got their names. During my research I found many whose names have been lost to history. A few of them are listed below along with their recipes.

The Mariner's Ghost
1. Add .75 oz of Dark Rum to shaker with ice.
2. Add .75 oz of Light Rum.
3. Puree a ripe Mango in a blender.
4. Add 1 oz of Mango puree.
5. Add .5 oz of Allspice Dram.
6. Add .5 oz of Lime Juice
7. Add 1 dash of Cointreau.
8. Shake and strain twice into Old Fashioned glass.
5. Garnish with a Mango Slice.

The Nut Bunny
1. Add 1.25 oz of Bourbon to shaker with ice.
2. Add .5 oz of Nocino.
3. Add .5 oz of Lemon Juice.
4. Add 3 dashes of Walnut Bitters.
5. Shake & strain over ice into an Old Fashion glass.
6. Garnish with a Rosemary or Lemon Peel.

The Tiger Paw
1. Add 2 oz of Citrus Vodka to shaker with ice.
2. Add 2 oz of Lemon Juice.
3. Add 1 tbsp of Sugar.
4. Shake and pour into a cup.
5. Fill with Orange Soda and stir.

The Red Dragon's Breath
1. Add 1 oz of DeKuyper Hot Damn Cinnamon Schnapps
2. Add 1 shot of Whiskey.
3. Mix in a shot glass and serve.

The Salty Dog
1. Rim a glass with salt and fill with ice.
2. Add 1.5 oz of Gin or Vodka.
3. Add 3 oz of Grapefruit Juice.
4. Garnish with a Lime or Cherry.

The Bulldog Smash
1. Add half a Lemon to shaker
2. Add half a Pitted Peach.
3. Add 6 to 8 Fresh Mint Leaves
4. Add 1 tsp of Sugar Cane Syrup.
4. Muddle the mixture.
5. Add 2 oz of Bourbon.
6. Add .75 oz of Cointreau
7. Fill your shaker with ice, shake, and strain into a glass.
8. Fill with crushed ice, garnish with a sprig of Mint.

The Trojan Horse
1. Add 8 oz of Guinness stout to a Pint Glass.
2. Add 8 oz of Coca-Cola.
3. Mix the Coke and Guinness.

Espresso Martini
1. Add 1.5 oz of Kahlua to a shaker with ice
2. Add 1 oz of Vodka.
3. Add 1 oz of Espresso.
4. Shake and strain into a Martini Glass.

Tokyo Tea (No Tea Involved)
1. Add .5 oz of Vodka to a shaker.
2. Add .5 oz of Rum.
3. Add .5 oz of Gin.
4. Add .5 oz of Tequila.
5. Add .5 oz of Triple Sec
6. Add .5 of Midori Melon Liqueur.
7. Shake & strain into small Highball Glass with ice.

The Last Word
1. Add .75 oz of gin to shaker with ice.
2. Add .75 oz of Green Chartreuse.
3. Add .75 oz of Maraschino Liqueur.
4. Add .75 oz of Lime Juice.
5. Shake and strain into Coupe Glass.

Jerry Bader
Author Biography

Jerry Bader is Senior Partner at MRPwebmedia.com a small media production company that specializes in Web video, audio, music, and sound design. He is responsible for developing concepts for clients' video campaigns, writing the scripts, and managing the production process. Over the years he's written over a hundred articles on marketing, and he's published three marketing books, four graphic novels, three biographies, and six children's books with more to come in each category.

Graphic Novels

Grist For The Mill
The Coffin Corner
The Method
The Comeuppance

Biographies

The Fixer
Beating The System
Organized Crime Queens, The Secret World of Female Gangsters
What Your Poison, How Cocktails Got Their Names

Children's Book (ZaZa Books For Kids)

Two Dragons Named Shoe
The Criminal McBride
The Town That Didn't Speak
The Bad Puppeteer
Mr. Bumbershoot, The Umbrella Man
The Ninth Inning

Marketing & Branding eBooks

What's The Big Idea?
Brand Universe
Double Take Marketing Techniques

Beating The System

Organized Crime Queens

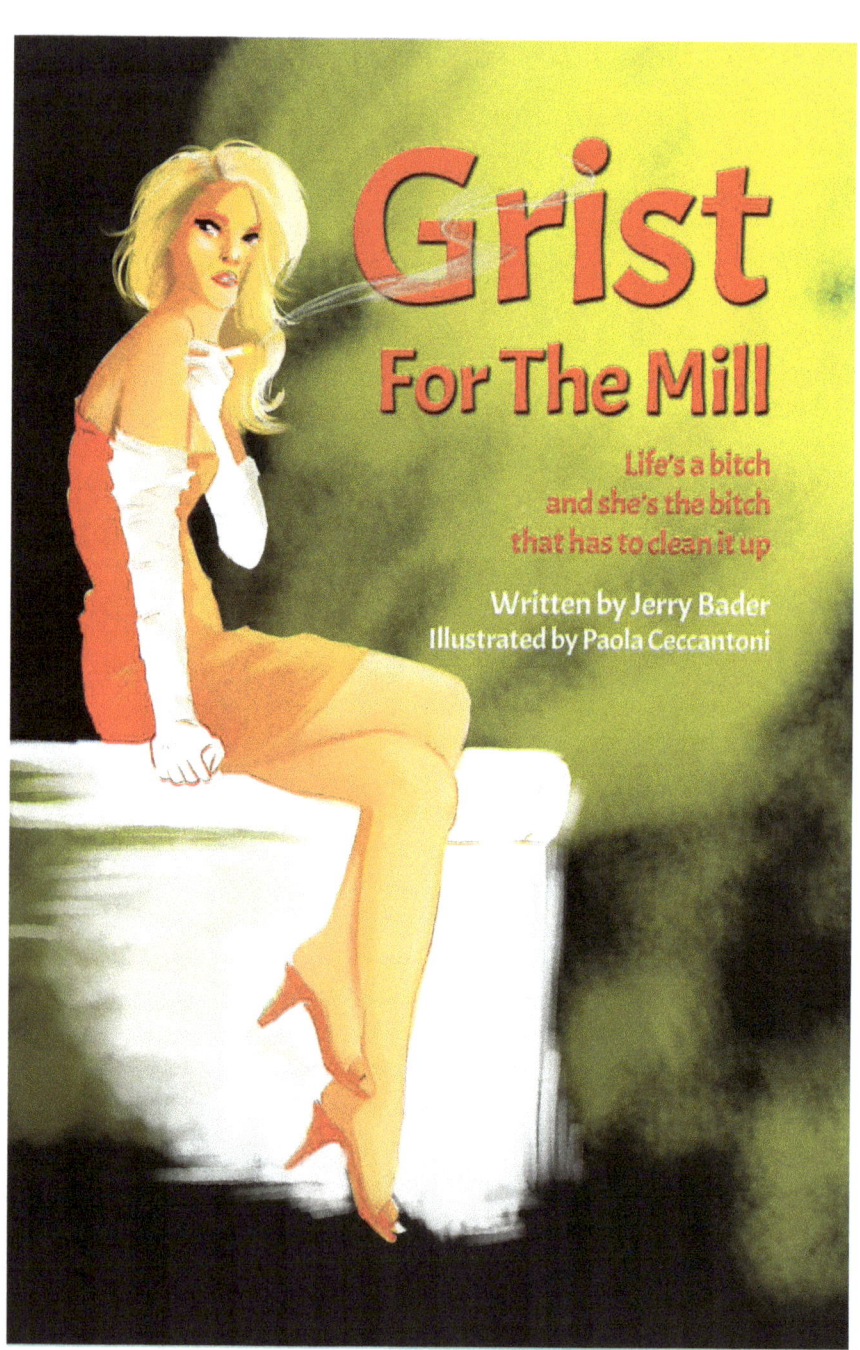

The Coffin Corner